Table of Contents

Introduction

Background Information for The 7 Habits of Highly Effective People by Stephen Covey

Do the principles in "The 7 Habits of Highly Effective People" still apply today, over 20 years after the book was first published? Yes, probably more than ever before. The bigger the problem or challenge, the more important is it to act with integrity, which is what the 7 Habits embody.

"The 7 Habits of Highly Effective People" was written by Stephen R. Covey and published in 1989. This summary is based on the 15th anniversary edition published in 2004.

Covey earned an MBA from Harvard Business School and a Doctorate in Religious Education from Brigham Young University. He does not, however, include his religious or political views in his writing.

Dr. Covey is the co-founder of Franklin-Covey. He has dedicated his life to helping people improve their personal and professional lives through self-awareness and interdependent, cooperative interactions. Covey has written numerous follow-up books to "The 7 Habits", listed at the end of this summary.

"The 7 Habits of Highly Effective People" was named one of the most influential business books on Forbes' list. It has sold over 15 million copies since its first publication and has been translated into 38 languages. Every year, over 100,000 people attend workshops on the 7 Habits.

Overall Summary of The 7 Habits of Highly Effective People by Stephen Covey

During the first 150 years of our country, success was based on the **Character Ethic**, traits such as integrity, humility, courage, justice, patience and modesty. After World War I, there was a shift to the **Personality Ethic.** Success became based on individual personality, image, attitude, behavior and skills.

While the Personality Ethic can certainly lead to success, it is secondary to the Character Ethic. It's quite possible to be successful, based on the elements of the Personality Ethic but be lacking in character. **True success and effectiveness begin with greatness in character**.

The 7 Habits exemplify strength of character. Covey calls it the **Inside-Out** approach. Begin on the inside in order to be successful on the outside.

As we develop our individual character, we grow from a level of dependence to independence to interdependence. In its simplest form, dependence is an infant depending on parents for survival. As we mature, however, relying on others to act for us is viewed as weak, and it is the lowest form of maturity.

Independence is a higher level of maturity, and is the strength and ability to take care of oneself. It means being proactive and doing things independently. However, that in itself is the weakness of independence – we act alone.

Interdependence is the highest form of maturity. It is working together, and valuing the differences in people. It is using the power of cooperation to achieve greater things than can be accomplished alone. Living the 7 Habits leads to interdependence.

Our character is defined by our habits – those consistent patterns of behavior that are often unconscious. Habits can be good or bad. Habits are powerful. They are deeply embedded and can be difficult to break. But, with knowledge (what to do and why), skill (how to do it), and desire (wanting to do it), we can create new habits that lead to success and effectiveness.

The 7 Habits of Highly Effective People are:

Private Victories – The first 3 Habits deal with Independence and Self-Improvement. It's the "I Can" view:

- **Habit 1** – Be Proactive
- **Habit 2** – Begin with the End in Mind
- **Habit 3** – Put First Things First

Public Victories – Habits 4, 5 and 6 lead to Cooperation and Interdependence. It's the "We Can" view:

- **Habit 4** – Think Win/Win
- **Habit 5** – Seek First to Understand, Then to be Understood
- **Habit 6** – Synergize

Renewal – The last Habit focuses on taking care of yourself, on a physical, mental, spiritual and social/emotional level:

- **Habit 7** – Sharpen the Saw

The 7 Habits build upon each other and are closely related. As you read this summary, keep in mind that **we face 3 types of problems in life**. Following the principles of the 7 Habits will help you approach problems and challenges in a more effective way. The types of problems and challenges are:

Direct – Problems that involve our behavior or our own weaknesses.Direct problems are within our Circle of Influence and are solved bythe **Private Victories** of Habits 1, 2 and 3;

Indirect – Problems that involve the behavior and weaknesses of others. Indirect problems are solved by increasing our Circle of Influence and through the **Public Victories** of Habits 4, 5 and 6;

No-Control – Problems we can do nothing about, including our past mistakes, some health conditions and accidents. No-control problems are dealt with by peacefully accepting the problem. As difficult as this is, it becomes easier through the **Renewal** of Habit 7.

Important People in The 7 Habits of Highly Effective People by Stephen Covey

Sandra Covey is Stephen Covey's wife, and she is referenced and quoted throughout the book. Sandra is passionate about the arts, having performed with the Mormon Tabernacle Choir as a teenager. In fact, she met her future husband while in Great Britain with the Choir. The Covey Center for Fine Arts, in Provo, Utah was named in her honor. Sandra is a member of the Brigham Young University President's Council. Along with her husband, she is coauthor of "The 7 Habits of Highly Effective Marriage" (2008).

Thomas Kuhn wrote "The Structure of Scientific Revolutions" and was an influential philosopher of science. He introduced the term "paradigm shift", which holds that almost all major breakthroughs in science begin with breaks in tradition – or a shift in paradigm. A scientific example of a paradigm shift is the shift from thinking the earth is at the center of the universe to the acceptance of the Sun being at the center. In his book, Covey presents an example of a paradigm shift in a simple optical illusion of an old woman and a young woman hidden in the same picture. He demonstrates how the same information can be viewed in different ways.

Mohandas (Mahatma) Ghandi is shown as an example of expanding your Circle of Influence to accomplish great things. Ghandi strived to bring peaceful change to India and is quoted as having said, *"They cannot take away our self respect if we do not give it to them."*

Anwar Sadat was President of Egypt from 1970 until his assassination in 1981. He is credited with the Egyptian-Israeli Peace Treaty. Sadat began his political career with a deep hatred for Israel. Through self-awareness, a Principle Center and effective leadership, he focused on his Circle of Influence and changed the behavior and attitudes of millions of people.

Viktor Frankl was a Jewish psychiatrist who survived imprisonment is a Nazi concentration camp. He strived to find meaning in life, even under the most extreme conditions. He is referenced throughout the book as an example of expanding one's Circle of Influence rather than dwelling on one's Circle of Concern.

Dag Hammarskjold was Secretary General of the United Nations. He once said, *"It is more noble to give yourself completely to one individual than to labor diligently for the salvation of the masses."* Covey uses this example in building trust and respect in relationships.

Roget Fisher and William Ury are the Harvard law professors who wrote "Getting to Yes". Their work on principled versus positional negotiation is in harmony with Covey's Win/Win approach. Fisher and Ury hold that the path to successful or principled negotiation is to focus on mutual gain.

Key Terms in The 7 Habits of Highly Effective People by Stephen Covey

Character Ethic is the philosophy that success stems from basic principles and values such as integrity, perseverance, humility and courage. Rewarding this manner of behavior was prevalent in the United States until World War I.

Personality Ethic is the philosophy that success is a result of an individual's skill, behavior, personality, image and attitude. It can be viewed as a selfish path to success as it focuses on the individual. After World War I, there was a shift from the Character Ethic to the Personality Ethic.

A **Paradigm Shift** is a major change in how something is viewed. This often reflects a major scientific advance that changes old views such as Einstein's Theory of Relativity or Darwin's Theory of Evolution. In Covey's opinion, not all paradigm shifts are positive, as exemplified by the shift from the Character Ethic to the Personality Ethic.

Habits are behaviors that express a person's character. They are deeply embedded patterns of behavior. Habits are simply defined as the tendency to act in a certain way. They are acquired by repetition. As Ralph Waldo Emerson said, *"What you are shouts so loudly in my ears that I cannot hear what you say."* Covey states that habits lead to our ultimate effectiveness or ineffectiveness. Importantly, they can be learned and unlearned. As the old adage goes, "Practice makes perfect."

The 3 Stages of Maturity: These are the stages of maturity that are relevant in personal interactions and to the 7 Habits. **Dependence** is the least mature stage of relying on others to act for us, such as a child depending on parents. **Independence** is a more mature stage of development and denotes being responsible for oneself. **Interdependence** is the highest level of maturity and involves working cooperatively with others to be more effective.

The 3 Types of Problems: Covey sorts problems into 3 distinct types. **Direct Control Problems** are problems we can solve through our own actions. **Indirect Control Problems** are problems we can solve by influencing others. **No-Control Problems**, however, are problems we can do nothing about.

Private Victory is realized in Habits 1, 2 and 3. These 3 Habits focus on self-improvement, self-discipline and self-mastery. They make Public Victory possible.

Public Victory is achieved through Habits 4, 5 and 6. These 3 Habits are characterized by emotional security, consideration, trust and confidence. Public Victory is accomplished by working together to reach mutually beneficial solutions.

Circle of Concern: The Circle of Concern includes all our problems, worries and concerns. Examples include the state of world affairs, one's health, our family's well-being and our work. We focus a lot of time and energy on our Circle of Concern, but some of the problems within our Circle of Concern are outside of our control.

Circle of Influence: Our Circle of Influenceis a smaller circle within our Circle of Concern. It encompasses the things we can control. Covey believes that focusing on the things we have the ability to change or control, rather than the things we cannot control, can increase our Circle of Influence and make us more effective.

Proactive: Proactivepeople focus on their Circle of Influence. They spend their time and energy on the things they can control and are therefore more responsible and effective.

Reactive: Reactive people focus on their Circle of Concern. They tend to overlook the things they can control and waste energy on the things they can't control.

Management is the ability to accomplish something. It involves control, rules and efficiency. Managers direct activities. Management is not the same as Leadership.

Leadership is recognizing what things need to be accomplished. It is involves vision, knowledge and strength of character. Leaders decide what activities should be pursued.

A **Personal Mission Statement** is a well thought out plan that encompasses your values, roles, goals and plans. It guides you and gives you a sense of purpose. An example taken from Covey's website is: *"I will be an optimist and enjoy everything that happens to me and everything I do. I want to be known by my family as a woman who loved and cared; by my friends as someone who was always there; by my employers as a fair, honest, responsible and hardworking individual. I want to ensure I respect anyone who ever worked for me and to earn his or her respect in return. I hope to live a life* *without regrets."*

Family Mission Statements are similar to Personal Mission Statements; however, they should include input from all family members. A Family Mission Statements helps solidify what matters most to a family. It provides a framework for decisions that affect the family, and it helps keep the family united in common values.

Organizational Mission Statements are also similar to Personal Mission Statements. They are a result of shared vision and values, and are based on respect and working together. To be effective, the mission statement must include input from all levels and members of an organization. In other words, the president of a company shouldn't decide the mission alone, otherwise, employees will not have an investment in it. Covey maintains that successful Organizational Mission Statements result in unity and commitment, and they are vital to success of an organization.

The Four Factors: Covey lists four factors that govern our actions and behaviors. **Security** is our sense of worth and personal strength. **Guidance** reflects the principles that give us direction in life. **Wisdom** represents our judgment, perspective and sense of balance. P**ower** means the ability and strength to act.

Principle Center: Covey describes a Principle Center or a Center of Values that guides our actions. With a Principle Center, effective decisions and actions are driven by principles; by our sense of security, guidance, wisdom and power; without reacting to emotion; and with a balanced view of the consequences.

Alternative Centers: Covey contrasts Alternative Centers with a Principle Center. With an Alternative Center (where our decisions are governed by the expectations/demands of a spouse, family, money, work, possession, pleasure, enemy, church, or self), decisions and actions are limited by what our spouse or others thinks, by what is best for the family or work, by image or status, by net worth, by comparisons or judgments, and by reactive impulses or negative energy. In short, decisions are not guided by principles. These Alternative Centers, therefore, result in unfulfilled potential and often resentment.

The 4 Generations of Time Management: Covey organizes management activities into 4 generations, ordered by effectiveness. The **1st Generation** includes notes and checklists. The **2nd Generation** involves looking ahead but may lack priority. The **3rd Generation** involves daily planning but may lack balance.
The **4th Generation** involves what Covey calls managing through principles and values. The 4th Generation is most effective and results in balance between quality of life and productivity.

Abundance Mentality is the belief that there is enough for everyone to succeed. It flows out of a sense of security, and results in deep satisfaction and fulfillment. Abundance Mentality recognizes unlimited possibilities.

The 5 Levels of Listening: Covey describes 5 Levels of Listening, which include ignoring, pretending to listen, selective listening, attentive listening, and empathic listening. **Ignoring** is not listening at all. **Pretending** to listen isn't listening either. **Selective listening** is hearing what we want to hear. **Attentive listening** is paying attention and focusing on what is being said. **Empathic Listening** is listening with the intent to understand both intellectually and emotionally. Emphatic Listening is listening from the other person's perspective, and it leads to trust in relationships.

Synergy is creative cooperation. It is defined as working together to produce something greater than could be accomplished alone. The whole is greater than the sum of individual parts.

Renewal is embodied in Habit 7. Simply put, it is taking care of oneself on a mental, physical, spiritual and emotional/social level. Renewal keeps your mind active and body healthy, clarifies your values, and provides security and satisfaction. Renewal leaves us with a sense of purpose. It makes all the other Habits possible.

The **Daily Private Victory** is described by Covey as an hour a day spent on Renewal of the mind, body and spirit. This can include exercise, reading, writing, reflecting, praying or meditating. This helps clear the mind, clarify your values, and refocus your goals. Covey contends this is a critical investment of your time, and that the Daily Private Victory will improve your overall effectiveness.

Major Themes in The 7 Habits of Highly Effective People by Stephen Covey

Inside-Out

Covey uses the term **Inside-Out** as a means to effectiveness. His approach to self-improvement focuses on character, principles and values – what's on the inside. In other words, to be successful on the outside, you must first begin on the inside, with your character.

While working on his doctorate degree, Covey noted a change in how success was viewed in the United States. Shortly after World War I, there was a paradigm shift from the Character Ethic to the Personality Ethic. Covey's stand is that the Character Ethic (an individual's character, principles and values) is primary to success, while the Personality Ethic (elements of one's personality and individual skill) is secondary to success.

Covey gives the example of trying to find your way in Chicago with a map of Detroit to guide you. Your secondary skills of map reading are important to your success, but without the primary element of having the correct map, you will never find your destination. Having the correct principles, or map, is the key to success and effectiveness.

Win/Win Negotiations

The Win/Win mentality of personal interactions is based on integrity, maturity and the belief in abundance (enough for everyone to succeed). In Win/Win negotiations, agreements and solutions are mutually beneficial to all parties.

Covey gives the example of a troubled company whose president was trying to make the workplace more cooperative. He thought the basic problem was that his employees were selfish and unwilling to cooperate. Upon closer examination, the problem was that the rewards system (a trip to Bermuda for the top employee) was causing competition among employees.

While the employees could accomplish more by working together, they were driven by a Win/Lose outcome – in order for one employee to win the trip, everyone else had to Lose. The alternative Win/Win view is that a Win for everyone, through cooperation, trust and respect for coworkers, is more successful and effective in the long-term.

Interdependence

Interdependence is the highest form of maturity in personal interactions. Rather than being dependent on others, or working independently, interdependence is working effectively with others. It embodies the Win/Win mentality, Empathic Listening and Synergy. Covey states that independent individuals can be productive, but strong leaders, effective team players and truly successful individuals function interdependently.

An example of interdependence in Covey's book is the beginning of the Atomic Energy Commission (AEC), which was established after World War II. The AEC was charged with controlling nuclear weapons and nuclear energy to promote world peace.

David Lilienthal was the first director of the AEC, and he found himself leading a very diverse, highly educated and headstrong group. He was criticized for acting slowly, but he took time to build strong and trusting relationships among the group members. The result was a respectful, cooperative, creative and synergistic approach to the challenges faced by the AEC.

Valuing differences is at the heart of interdependent interactions. Interdependence begins with building trust and respect in relationships. As exemplified in the AEC, the results can be extraordinary. Living the 7 Habits leads to interdependence and effectiveness.

II.

Detailed Summary

Summary of The 7 Habits of Highly Effective People: Habit 1 – Be Proactive

"Act or be acted upon."

Self-awareness is a human trait that allows us to learn from our past, and to *"make and break old habits".* We can clearly see ourselves and others, and analyze our own thought processes. Our self-awareness ultimately affects how we behave and how effective we are.

Covey uses the example of a crazy carnival mirror to demonstrate self-awareness. Often, distorted views of ourselves and others are really just projections of character weakness, rather than true reflections of who we are.

There are 3 widely accepted theories that determine human nature, or who we are. They can lead, independently or in concert, to self-fulfilling prophecies that often result in ineffectiveness.

- **Genetic**– We are the way we are due to our grandparents, our genes, our DNA.
- **Psychic** – We are the way we are due to our parents, our childhood experiences, our fears, our emotions.
- **Environment** – We are the way we are due to our boss, our spouse, our children, the economy, government, world instability.

It may seem like we have little to no control over these factors, but in addition to self-awareness, we also possess:

- **Imagination** – We can create something in our minds that is better than the present reality;
- **Conscience** – We know right from wrong, and that there are consequences to our actions;

* **Independent Will** – We can act based on our self-awareness, imagination and conscience.

Therefore, we are **proactive**, and can take responsibility for our own lives. In short, *"Our behavior is a function of our decisions, not our conditions."* If we choose to blame others for our conditions, we become **reactive**.

Covey states, *"Proactive Peopleare driven by values – carefully thought about, selected and internalized values"* while *"Reactive People are driven by feelings, by circumstances, by conditions, by their environment."*

To demonstrate, consider the difference between **Reactive Language** and **Proactive Language:**

Reactive Language:

There's nothing I can do.

That's just the way I am.

He makes me so mad.

They won't allow that.

I have to do that.

I can't.

I must.

If only.

Proactive Language:

Let's look at our alternatives.

I can choose a different approach.

I control my own feelings.

I can create an effective presentation.

I will choose an appropriate response.

I choose.

I prefer.

I will.

While there are things in life that can hurt us physically, emotionally and economically, it's really how we respond that matters. Our character is shaped by difficult and challenging experiences. Just look at the following examples.

1) We've heard stories of, or perhaps even known, someone who was dying who remained optimistic until the end – someone who touched our lives through their courage and strength; who lived a life of character, service, love and appreciation; who at heart was proactive and self-aware.

2) Covey writes about prisoners of war, surviving extreme conditions of torture and years of captivity. What is it that survivors had in common? They were proactive even in the face of conditions they could not control. Covey gives the example of Viktor Frankl, a Jewish psychiatrist and Holocaust survivor. He became an inspiration to other prisoners. While he was imprisoned in a Nazi concentration camp, he helped other prisoners with depression, and he remained optimistic by focusing on his love for his wife and envisioning teaching students.

3) Covey also shares an experience that is highly **relevant in today's economic climate.** Years ago, he worked with several companies in the midst of an economic recession.

They were discouraged with facing the prospects of layoffs and widespread unemployment. They looked at their future prospects and became even more depressed, as things would likely get worse before they got better. Finally, they got to the proactive stage and asked, "What are we going to do?" They resolved to improve business by carefully managing and reducing costs, and working to increase their market share. They focused on the positive and tried to make better business decisions.

While this may seem like only positive thinking, it's really the difference between being proactive and reactive. **Proactive people take responsibility, face reality, and choose a positive response to difficult situations**, even those that are outside their control.

It is important, while dealing with our problems, to look at our **Circle of Concern**, the collection of problems we face and things we worry about. Within that circle, there is a **Circle of Influence**, including all the things that we have control over and can do something about. *"At the very heart of our Circle of Influence is our ability to make and* *keep commitments."*

Proactive people keep their commitments and they use positive energy to increase their Circle of Influence. They make promises and keep them. They set goals and work to achieve them.

Reactive people focus on their Circle of Concern. While proactive people focus on what they can do, reactive people focus only on problems and things they have no control over. They feel victimized, and their Circle of Influence shrinks.

As we try to solve problems by focusing on our Circle of Influence, we must also keep in mind that there are **consequences** and **mistakes** to our actions. Negative consequences and mistakes can lead to regrets that are outside our Circle of Influence.

Our response to a mistake affects us deeply. We know it's best to immediately own up to a mistake, correct it, and learn from it. Sometimes it may seem easier to cover up a mistake, thereby making a second mistake and creating a bigger problem.

A **reactive response to a mistake** can lead to self-deception, lies, self-justification, and deep injury.

A **proactive response to a mistake** can actually turn a mistake or failure into a success.

As you work on Habit 1, Covey suggests you **try these exercises**.

1)   For one day, carefully listen to your language and to the language of others around you. Is it proactive or reactive?

2)   Think about a situation that is coming up, one to which you might respond reactively. Now think about your Circle of Influence. How might you respond proactively instead?

3)   Think of a problem, either personal or work-related. Is it a direct, an indirect, or a no-control problem? What is the first step to solving the problem, the first step within your Circle of Influence?

4)   Keeping in mind your Circle of Influence, try a 30-day test of proactivity. Make small commitments and keep them. Focus your energy on the positive. Don't blame. If you make a mistake, admit it, fix it and learn from it.

Habit 1 – Be Proactive, and lead a life of self-awareness. This can be "*very hard to accept emotionally, especially if we have had years and years of explaining our misery in* *the name of circumstance or someone else's behavior*." However, in the words of Eleanor Roosevelt, *"no one can hurt you without your consent."* You control your own destiny, and being proactive is the first step to success.

Summary of The 7 Habits of Highly Effective People: Habit 2 – Begin with the End in Mind

Sometimes *"what matters most gets buried under layers of pressing problems, immediate concerns."*

A striking way to think about Beginning with the End in Mind is to **think about your own funeral**.

- What do you want your family, friends, coworkers and community to remember about you?
- What character traits, contributions and achievements will have mattered?
- Did you make a difference in the lives of others?

In thinking about your own funeral, **your definition of success may change.** Through self-awareness, you may find that you have deep habits that are unworthy, and are not aligned with what you really value.

If you really think about the end of your own life and what will have mattered most, you will clarify your fundamental values. As you move through your life, **your behavior** – today's, tomorrow's, next month's, next year's – should all contribute to the vision you have of the end. Are you going in the right direction?

It's easy to get caught up in an activity trap. Life is busy. Life can be stressful. We have to work hard to succeed. But, *"it is possible to be busy – very busy – without being very effective."*

As you proactively plan out the important events of your life, there is first a mental creation and then a physical creation to what we do. As Covey states, *"All things are created twice."*

Take the example of building a home. You first think of what you want in a home. Then you start building it with a design and construction. It's really created three times – deciding what is important and needed, followed by a design or set of rules for the building, and finally the actual construction.

This is also true for a business or a family. **You first define what you want to accomplish,** Beginning with the End in Mind. The next steps involve using your Circle of Influence to accomplish your goals.

Habit 2 is based on **leadership and management.** They are **notthe same things**! Leadership must come first. Leadership is the vision of what we want to accomplish. Management is how we get there and how effective we are.

"Management is doing things right; Leadership is doing the right things."

-Peter Drucker and Warren Bennis

A good way to put your life into perspective is to develop a **Personal Mission Statement**. Take some time to think about what's important to you. This can't be written overnight, and it doesn't end with writing it. It deserves careful thought and introspection.

After you've written your statement, review it occasionally, and make changes to improve it. With your Personal Mission Statement, you have a vision that directs your life effectively. When you get off track, you can self-correct

Your Personal Mission Statement **guides your long-term and short-term goals**. It touches on your values, character, and what you want to contribute in life. It is *"the basis for making major, life-directing decisions, the basis for making daily decisions in the midst of the circumstances and emotions that affect our lives."* It gives you **strength under stress and ever-present change**.

It helps to break your Personal Mission Statement down into the **different roles** that are important to you. Then **set the goals** needed be successful in each of your roles. For example, your roles as a parent, spouse or friend are all different and separate from your roles at work or in your community.

Setting long-term goals for each of your roles keeps balance in your life. You are proactive rather than reactive because you Begin with the End in Mind.

As you write your Personal Mission Statement, look at your Circle of Influence. What are the **values** that decide what is important to you? Use your **self-awareness** and

conscience to guide you, and use your **imagination** to create the ending you want.

It is also helpful to have a **Family Mission Statement** and an **Organization Mission Statement** for work. There are entire books that cover effectiveness of these more complex groups. The main idea is that everyone in the family or organization needs to be involved in deciding the mission.

Writing a Family or Orgainization Mission Statement takes time, skill, thought, patience, shared vision, shared values and sincerity. When done properly, a group's Mission Statement **creates unity and commitment** from all members because they all **share the vision** of what they want to accomplish together.

Now, going back to your own Personal Mission Statement, at the **Center** of your **Circle of Influence** is the source of your **security, guidance, wisdom and power.** These four factors are very important in your Personal Mission Statement.

- **Security** is your personal strength, sense of worth, identity and emotional anchor.
- **Guidance** is your sense of direction and the values that govern your behavior.
- **Wisdom** is your sense of balance and judgment in making decisions.
- **Power** is your strength or ability to accomplish something.

When these four factors are balanced, the results are positive. When they are not balanced, we can lose sight of Beginning with the End in Mind, and the results are negative.

Covey states that we all have a **Center of Values** within our Circle of Influence. Your Center guides your actions. With a **Principle Center**, a Center based on integrity and ethics, there is balance of security, guidance, wisdom and power. There is a solid foundation for making decisions.

These are the 4 factors that drive your decisions and actions if you have a **Principle Center:**

Security:

- Your security is based on correct, unchanging values.
- Your values are validated through your experiences.
- You function with strength and consistency.

Guidance:

- You are guided by your values.

- You use data to make meaningful decisions.
- Your decisions reflect short-term and long-term goals.
- You stand apart from emotions of a situation and look at the balanced whole.
- You are proactive and determine the best solution based on your values.

Wisdom:

- Your judgment is guided by consequences.
- You see and act differently than the largely-reactive world.
- You view the world in terms of what you can do for the world.
- You are proactive and seek to serve.
- You see opportunities for learning and contribution.

Power:

- Your power comes from your principles and their consequences.
- You are self-aware and proactive.
- You act interdependently.
- Your decisions are not driven by finances or limitations.

Now, take a look at the following examples of **Alternative Centers**, Centers guided by external factors rather than integrity or ethics. See how easy it is to get off course, even with the best of intentions, such as being centered on your spouse, family or church.

Spouse Center: Your security is based on how your spouse treats you. You feel disappointment if your spouse disagrees with you. You feel threatened by outside forces. Your decisions are guided by what is best for your relationship. You are limited by weaknesses in your spouse and yourself.

Family Center: Your security is based on family acceptance and expectations. Self-worth is based on family reputation. Your decisions are guided by what is good for the family, or what family members want. You are limited by your view of family models and traditions.

Money Center: Your self-worth is determined by your net worth. Profit guides your decisions. You view of life is through moneymaking, resulting in poor judgment. Your power is governed by money and limited vision.

Work Center: You define yourself by your work. Your decisions are based on work expectations. Your work is your life. Your power is limited by your boss, work place, and the ability or inability to complete work.

Possession Center: Your security is based on social status and possessions. You compare what you have to others. Your decisions are based on protecting, increasing or displaying your possessions. You view the world in term of economic and social status. Your power is limited by what you can buy and your social standing.

Pleasure Center: Your security is short-lived and depends on your environment. Your decisions are guided by what gives you the most pleasure. Your view is "what's in it for me?" You have little power or focus.

Friend Center: Your security depends on the opinions of others. Your decisions are guided by what others think. Your view of the world is through a social lens. You are limited by your social comfort zone and you may be unreliable.

Enemy Center: Your security is driven by your enemy's actions. You seek the like-minded. You always wonder what your enemy is doing. Your decisions are guided by what hurts your enemy, and this is counter-dependent. Your judgment is distorted, and you are paranoid and defensive. You have little power and it comes from anger, envy, resentment and vengeance. This negative energy is destructive.

Church Center: Your security is based on church activity and religious comparisons. You are guided by how others judge you with regard to religious teaching. You view the world in terms of believers and non-believers, right and wrong. Your perceived power is based on your position in church.

Self Center: Your security is constantly changing. Your decisions are guided by "what's in it for me?" You view the world by how it affects you and only you. Your power is limited by your resources. While you are independent, you function without interdependency.

Obviously, your Center affects your decisions, your actions and your motivations. A person with a **Principle Center** can **find balance in a situation and come up with the best solution** to a problem. Keep in mind that principles don't react to change or stress. They aren't emotional. They are constant fundamental truths.

With a Principle Center, you have the values to make the right decisions no matter what the outside forces may be. You know that there are consequences to your decisions, but when you use the correct principles, you act wisely and effectively. What you choose to do **contributes to your values and the quality of your life.**

When facing a problem with a Principle Center, you make the decision to act and you know your decision is effective because it is based on your values and core principles.

You are independent and can therefore be interdependent. You are comfortable with your decisions. In short, you are **proactive and effective**.

As you work on Habit 2, Covey suggests you **try these exercises**.

- Think about your own funeral, and write down how you'd like to be remembered by family, friends, work and community.
- Write down the important roles in your life. Are you satisfied with this image?
- Begin to develop your Personal Mission Statement.
- Look at the different Alternative Centers. Which ones do you identify with? Is there a pattern that explains your behavior? Are you comfortable with your Center?
- Look for inspirational quotes or ideas that will help in writing your Personal Mission Statement.
- Think about an upcoming project. Begin with the End in Mind, and decide what the end results should be.
- Share the ideas behind Habit 2 with family or at work, and suggest a group Mission Statement.

Habit 2 – Begin with the End in Mind, and lead your life with a Principle Center. Use your Personal Mission Statement to guide you. In the end, what will you have contributed? This approach *"forces you to think through your priorities deeply, carefully and to align your behavior with your beliefs."*

Summary of The 7 Habits of Highly Effective People: Habit 3 – Put First Things First

....

"The successful person has the habit of doing the things failures don't like to do."

-E.M. Gray

There are entire books and courses devoted totime management. How you manage your time is directly linked to how effective you are. Ask yourself the following questions.

- Is there something that you could do (that you aren't doing now) that would make a positive impact in your **personal life**?
- Likewise, is there something that you could do that would make a positive impact in your **professional life**?

"Putting First Things First" is effective time management. It takes into account your self-awareness, imagination, conscience and adds **independent-will**. It is your discipline and ability to make decisions and choose to act on them.

To better understand how to manage your time effectively, let's look at the**4 Generations of Time Management.** The first 3 approaches to Time Management would appear to be effective, but it's really the 4th approach that results in effective personal time management.

1st Generation of Time Management: Includes notes and checklists, all your to-do's. 1st generation managers have little ability to prioritize. There is often little correlation between what's on their list and what their ultimate goals are.

2nd Generation of Time Management: Includes calendars and looking ahead. 2nd generation managers assume more control by planning, but the activities they schedule may still have little priority.

3rd Generation of Time Management: Includes daily planners and setting goals. 3rd generation managers plan each day and prioritize, but daily planning can miss the bigger picture. There may be no balance of priorities, and a tendency to over-schedule.

4th Generation of Time Management: Includes managing through personal principles and values, with a clear vision of your mission. There is balance between your productivity and quality of life. 4th generation managers focus on *"preserving and enhancing relationships and on accomplishing results"*.

Now let's look at the types of activities we typically need to manage, from the most urgent to the most trivial.

The 4 Quadrants of Activities

Quadrant 1: Important and Urgent Activities:

- Crisis Management
- Pressing Problems
- Deadlines

Quadrant 2: Important and Not Urgent Activities:

- Prevention
- Relationships
- Opportunities
- Planning
- Recreation

Quadrant 3: Unimportant and Urgent Activities:

- Interruptions
- Some calls, mail, reports
- Some meetings
- Immediate problems
- Popular activities

Quadrant 4: Unimportant and Not Urgent Activities:

- Trivia
- Busy work
- Some mail, calls
- Time wasters
- Pleasant activities

Effective people operate mostly in Quadrant 2 – the Important but Not Urgent activities. Effective people spend little time in Quadrants 3 and 4, and they shrink stressful Quadrant 1 activities.

We can't avoid every crisis, and we know that deadlines are a reality. We all find ourselves in Quadrant 1 at times. However, if you operate mostly in **Quadrant 1**, Urgent and Important activities, you are always **dealing with crises and putting out fires**.

In Quadrant 1, you may think you're being effective but you run the risk of burnout and stress. Your problems often become bigger and they can dominate your life. In the end, you feel beaten up, and may try to escape to Quadrant 4 activities.

People who operate mostly in **Quadrant 3**, Urgent but Not Important activities, may think they are effective. They may even think they are in Quadrant 1. But, they are really **reacting** to everything around them, and their priorities are based on the expectations of others.

Quadrant 3 is characterized by short-term focus. Goals and plans are often worthless. Individuals that operate mostly in Quadrant 3 often have shallow or fractured relationships. They are **busy and stressed**, but despite all their work, they are **ineffective**.

People who operate in **Quadrant 4**, Not Urgent and Not Important activities, are **irresponsible**. They are often immature, dependent on others, and have difficulty holding a job. They waste their time on trivial matters, and are completely **ineffective**.

"Quadrant 2is the heart of effective personal management." These activities are all the things we know we need to do, but don't get around to because they aren't urgent.

Examples of Quadrant 2 activities include building and strengthening relationships, writing a Personal Mission Statement, long-term planning, preparation, preventative maintenance, spending quality time with family and friends, and exercising.

Quadrant 2 is where we **find opportunities**. Think back to the questions at the beginning of the chapter. **What could you do to improve your personal or professional life?** The answer probably lies in Quadrant 2 – Important but Not Urgent activities.

Quadrant 2 activities can make a tremendous positive impact on your life. *"Our effectiveness takes quantum leaps when we do them."*

It takes saying "NO" to activities in Quadrants 3 and 4, to find time to function in Quadrant 2. Effective people know how to **proactively say "YES" to important activities.** They also know how to say **"NO" to less important activities**, even when they appear urgent.

Covey asks: *"If you were to fault yourself in one of three areas, which would it be:*

- *The inability to **prioritize**;*
- *The inability or desire to **organize** around those priorities; or*
- *The lack of **discipline** to... stay with your priorities?"*

Most people say, *"lack of discipline"*, but Covey thinks the fault is actually *"lack of priorities"*. This goes back to **Beginning with the End in Mind**. It's hard to say "NO" to the popularity of Quadrant 3 or the pleasure of Quadrant 4, unless you Begin with the End in Mind.

Looking back at Habit 2, **Quadrant 2 activities are rooted in a Principle Center.** For example, if you are centered on spouse, money, pleasure or self, you end up in Quadrants 1 and 3. You are impulsive and reactive. However, if you have a Principle Center, your **priorities grow out of your values** and are deeply rooted in your being.

There are **6 important criteria** to be an **effective Quadrant 2** organizer.

- **Coherence** – There should be harmony and integrity between your mission, roles, goals, priorities, plans, desires and discipline.
- **Balance** – Identify your roles and keep them in sight. For instance, don't neglect your health or family for work.
- **Focus** – Organize your life by weeks. You can adjust priorities daily, but the goals for your week should be clearly planned.
- **A "People" Dimension** – Think in terms of **effectiveness with people, and efficiency with time.** You can't always rush people. Spend time on your relationship.
- **Flexibility** – Your plan is your servant, not your master. Flexibility lets you handle unanticipated events and to enjoy life because you have a full week to accomplish your goals.
- **Portability** – Find a planning system that you can carry with you. (This is quite easy in today's world of electronics and information.) Always have important data with you.

Write your Personal Mission Statement in your planner so you can refer to it. Find a place for your roles, and your short-term and long-term goals. Then schedule time to achieve your goals.

"The key is not to prioritize what's on your schedule,

but to schedule your priorities."

For Weekly Scheduling, it's important to start with your roles, make goals for them, make plans to meet those goals, and delegate/schedule to put those plans in action.

Delegating increases your effectiveness. Once you spend the time to train someone else, they become responsible for the results. For this to work well, there must be a clear understanding of the desired results, guidelines to complete the work, resources to accomplish the task, accountability and evaluation of the results, and consequences for success or failure.

"Delegation is perhaps the best indicator of

effective management."

As you work on Habit 3, Covey suggests you **try these exercises**.

- Identify an activity in Quadrant 2 that you have neglected. One that will make a positive impact on your life. Make a plan to do it.
- Estimate the time you spend in each of the Quadrants. Are you satisfied with this? Do you need to change?
- Make a list of responsibilities that you could delegate. What is needed to start delegating?
- Organize your next week. Start with your roles and goals. At the end of the week, evaluate how well you did.
- Commit to start organizing your weeks.
- Use the 4th Generation of Time Management in your planning.
- Focus on Quadrant 2 activities.

Habit 3 – Put First Things First. Strive to work in Quadrant 2. This allows you to *"look through the lens of importance rather than urgency"*. Manage your time through a Principle Center, which balances your mission, roles and goals, and recognizes the importance of relationships.

Summary of The 7 Habits of Highly Effective People: Habit 4 – Think Win/Win

....

"Anything less than Win/Win in an interdependent

reality is a poor second best ..."

Habit 4 is **effective interpersonal leadership.** This is the beginning of interdependence. In interpersonal leadership, there are *6 types of interactions.*

- **Win/Win** – Agreements and solutions are mutually beneficial for all. This view holds that life is cooperative, not competitive. Success is not achieved at the expense of others. There is enough for everyone to succeed.

- **Win/Lose** – "If I win, you lose." This approach is about power and position. Examples include peer groups that reject or accept; athletics or games with a zero sum outcome; academics where good grades are required for success; and competition in the business world.

- **Lose/Win** – The opposite of Win/Lose. There are no standards, demands, expectations, or vision. Lose/Win people seek strength from popularity, but have little courage and are easily intimidated. This approach to negotiations can result in buried resentments leading to delayed responses (illness, rage, low self-esteem, poor quality of relationships).

- **Lose/Lose** – Results when 2 Win/Lose people interact. It is characterized by stubbornness and can be vindictive. It is the view of dependent people with no direction who are often miserable and want everyone else to be miserable.

- **Win** – Only winning matters. This view is independent. While everyone is responsible for themselves, this approach can negatively impact long-term relationships.

- **Win/Win or No Deal** – This is a higher order of Win/Win, and it is interdependent. The solution is either agreeable to everyone – Win/Win; or you agree to disagree – No Deal. With No Deal as an option, *"you feel liberated because you have no need to manipulate people, to push your own agenda."*

Which of these is best? It depends on the situation.

Win/Win or No Deal is highly interdependent and leads to high levels of trust in relationships. So, it would appear to always be the best approach. However, Win/Lose or Win approaches can sometimes help business by creating healthy competition. Other times they may hurt business by leading to resentments that affect future negotiations.

When thinking about the well-being of your family or in an emergency situation, Win may be critical. In a relationship, it's sometimes helpful to give a little and let a loved one win, Lose/Win.

Another way to view these approaches in negotiation is through levels of consideration and courage.

- **Win/Win** is high in consideration and high in courage.
- **Win/Lose** is high in courage but low in consideration.
- **Lose/Win** is high in consideration but low in courage.
- **Lose/Lose** is low in both consideration and courage.

Win/Win invokes self-awareness, imagination, conscience, and independent-will. It takes courage and consideration. Win/Win requires vision and being proactive as well as having security, guidance, wisdom and power from a Principle Center. Win/Win **starts with character**.

There are 3 essential character traits for Win/Win:

- **Integrity** – honesty and our innermost values;
- **Maturity** –balance of courage and consideration;
- **Abundance Mentality–** the view that there is plenty for everyone to succeed.

In applying these character traits to negotiations, you build. From trusting relationships come **Win/Win agreements**. For a successful Win/Win agreement, there must be:

- **Desired results** – what needs to be accomplished;
- **Guidelines** – how should it be done (policies, principles);
- **Resources** – people, money, technical support to accomplish the goal;

- **Accountability** – evaluation of performance;
- **Consequences** – what happens upon success or failure.

With these elements, it is easy to measure success because the agreement is up front and it is understood by all parties. There are consequences to performance such as financial gain or loss; recognition, approval and respect; future opportunities; and increase or decrease in responsibilities.

Finally, in thinking about Win/Win, there is a **4-step process** to success.

- Seek and **understand the problem** from the other point of view.
- Identify everyone's **needs and concerns**.
- Determine the **results needed** to reach the successful solution.
- Identify **other possible ways** to get results.

As you work on Habit 4, Covey suggests you **try these exercises**.

- Think of an upcoming interaction in which an agreement needs to be reached. Commit to balance your courage and consideration in negotiating.
- Make a list of the things that keep you from applying the Win/Win approach more often. What can be done within your Circle of Influence to improve this?
- Think of a relationship where you'd like to make a Win/Win agreement. Put yourself in the other person's shoes. Write down what you think that person's winning solution is. What is your winning solution? Ask the other person if he/she is willing to work to reach a Win/Win solution.
- Think of 3 relationships in your life. How could you improve the trust level in each?
- Think deeply about your own interactions. Are they based on Win/Lose thinking? If so, how does this affect your interactions? Why do you behave this way? Does this approach serve you well?
- Think of someone who is a role model for Win/Win thinking. Someone who is focused on mutual benefit. Watch and learn from this person.

Habit 4 – Think Win/Win. Win/Win is about interdependence, working together and **high-trust relationships**. Win/Win is built on integrity, maturity and the Abundance Mentality. Success in Habit 4 is achieved through Habits 5 and 6.

Summary of The 7 Habits of Highly Effective People: Habit 5 – Seek First to Understand, Then to be Understood

"If you want to interact effectively with me,

to influence me...

you first need to understand me."

Covey says that **Habit 5 is the single most important principle** he has learned! It "*is the key to effective interpersonal communication.*"

While we take years to learn to communicate, most of us rarely learn to listen with the intent of truly understanding another person's point of view. Most people listen with the intent of replying, not understanding. We usually listen at one of 4 levels.

- **Ignoring** – Not listening at all.
- **Pretending** – "Uh-huh. Right." Still not really listening.
- **Selective** – Hearing only what we want to hear.
- **Attentive** – Paying attention and focusing on the words.

There is a **5th level of listening** – **Empathic Listening**, "*listening with the intent to understand"*. It means listening through another person's perspective, seeing the world through their eyes, understanding their view, and understanding how they feel. This **doesn't mean you have to agree**with the person. It does mean that you "*fully, deeply, understand that person, emotionally as well as intellectually.*"

Experts say that we communicate 10% with words, 30% with sounds or how we say the words, and 60% by behavior or body language. So, our understanding is limited when we listen to only words.

Empathic Listening is listening with your ears, eyes and heart. Covey says the greatest need of humans is first survival, followed by the need to be understood and appreciated.

Empathic Listeningcan be risky. You become vulnerable because *"you open yourself up to be influenced"*. In order to have influence, you need to understand the other person, which means they can influence you. But, with Empathic Listening comes **great trust**, which leads to cooperation and interdependence.

As we listen, we usually **respond in one of 4 ways**.

- We agree or disagree – **evaluate**.
- We ask questions from our view – **probe**.
- We give a solution from our perspective – **advise**.
- We try to figure out the problem from our view – **interpret**.

In other words, we aren't actually listening to the other person's perspective.

The **skills** needed for Empathic Listeningare, from least to greatest effect:

- **Mimicking content** - repeating what someone just said, but this can be insulting;
- **Rephrasing the content**- a little more effective but is still just using words;
- **Reflecting feeling** - paying attention to what someone says and feels;
- **Rephrasing and Reflecting Feelings** - the most effective skill, involves rephrasing what you've heard and paying attention to what the other person feels.

Look at the following example given in Covey's book. It's a dialogue between a father and son.

Son: "Boy, Dad, I've had it! School is for the birds!"

Dad: "You've had it. You think school is for the birds." *(mimic)*

Dad: "You don't want to go to school anymore." *(rephrase)*

Dad: "You're feeling really frustrated." *(reflect feeling)*

Dad: "You're really frustrated about school." *(rephrase and reflect)*

Which response do you think will be the most effective for Dad's interaction with his son?

Empathic Listening often takes time. People resent being rushed or manipulated. They may need time to open up about a problem. However, if you are patient and **listen to understand**, people will open up. While this takes time, it doesn't take as much time as correcting a misunderstanding.

Being understood is the 2nd part of Habit 5, and it's very important in reaching a Win/Win. Being understood also requires consideration and courage. **Presenting your ideas clearly and with integrity**, with the **other person's perspective** in mind, **gives your ideas more strength**. This approach requires skill and practice.

As you work on Habit 5, Covey suggests you **try these exercises**.

- Think of a relationship you have that is low on trust. Try to understand the situation from the other person's view. The next time you talk to this person, listen to understand. What do you hear? Do you really understand the person's point of view?
- Share the Empathic Listening idea with someone close to you. Tell them you want to work on your listening skills with them and would like feedback in a week. How did the other person feel about your approach?
- Find a situation where you can watch people communicating. Cover your ears and just watch. What emotions are being communicated?
- The next time you respond by probing, evaluating, advising or interpreting, stop and apologize. Start over.
- The next time you give a presentation, describe the other point of view first. Then seek to have your point of view understood.

Habit 5 – Seek First to Understand, Then to be Understood. We all want to be understood. Habit 5 expands your Circle of Influence because as you listen to understand, you can be influenced. Therefore, you **increase your ability to influence.** By Empathic Listening, many problems can be prevented because it reduces misunderstandings and **inspires trust and loyalty**.

Summary of The 7 Habits of Highly Effective People: Habit 6 – Synergize

"Synergy is the highest activity in all life – the true test...

of all the other habits put together."

Synergy means **cooperative action**, or working together to produce something greater than the sum of individual parts. It means $1 + 1 =$ more than 2, sometimes much more.Synergy **combines Win/Win** outcomes and **Empathic Listening** with our self-awareness, imagination, conscience, and independent will. *"What results is almost miraculous."*

Synergy opens new options. **All parties benefit.** It is characterized by excitement and positive energy.

Can you think of a synergistic experience you've had? Think of a team spirit or an emergency situation, where everyone put away their pride and egos, and worked together. This probably brings to mind an amazing sense of accomplishment. While synergy may be unusual to you, it can be created in your daily life.

Think of synergy in the context of a classroom or in business. It is a hunger for learning something **new and exciting**. It is the drive to be **creative** and produce something **meaningful**.

Think of synergy in the context of communication. It is **key to cooperation** and Win/Win outcomes **(Habit 4).** When there is a disagreement, there is a **real effort to understand (Habit 5**). Look at the following examples of communication in relation to synergy.

- **Low-trust communication** is not synergistic. It is defensive and protective, and results in Win/Lose or Lose/Lose outcomes.

- **Respectful communication** is mature but still not synergistic. It is polite but not empathic. It may produce some success but creativity may be missing. It often results in compromise. $1 + 1 = 1\frac{1}{2}$.
- **Synergistic communication** is high in trust and creativity. It is interdependent. The solution is better than first expected. $1 + 1 =$ more than 2, often much more than 2.

Synergy "*requires enormous personal security and*

openness and a spirit of adventure."

Synergy moves away from the "either/or" mentality and focuses on Win/Win. It also values differences. A truly effective person has the **humility to see his/her own limitations and to appreciate the knowledge, ability and strength in others!**

To better understand synergy and how to create it, think of the **opposite of synergy**. Think of the negative energy that can be spent on a problem when there is rivalry, low trust, conflict, back stabbing, second guessing, and manipulation. It's **ineffective**.

Synergy is powerful against these types of negative forces that work against your effectiveness. The positive forces of synergy are "*reasonable, logical, conscious and economic*". The negative forces against synergy are "*emotional, illogical, unconscious, and social/psychological*".

Now, think about the climate in your family or work place. Is it synergistic? Is it positive or negative? Do members feel safe or unsafe in expressing themselves? Is there respect or disrespect? You can change the climate to one of more respect, trust and synergy.

To create synergy, you use the previous 5 habits to work against negative forces.

Habit 1 – Be Proactive

Habit 2 – Begin with the End in Mind

Habit 3 – Put First Things First

Habit 4 – Think Win/Win

Habit 5 – Seek First to Understand, Then to be Understood

You start by involving people in the problem, so they are an important part of the solution. You strategize a solution together. You foster teamwork, from which grows unity and creativity. The results are new and shared goals, and a synergistic Win/Win outcome.

As you work on Habit 6, Covey suggests you **try these exercises**.

- Think of someone who sees things differently than you do. Can you value their different views? How could your differences lead to synergistic interactions?
- Think of people who irritate you. Do they have different views that could lead to synergy, if you had more security and valued their differences?
- Think of a situation that needs more teamwork. What conditions are needed for synergy? How can you create those conditions?
- The next time you have a disagreement, try to understand the other person's view. Try to address their concerns in a creative and synergistic way.

Habit 6 – Synergize. Synergy is the *"crowning achievement of all the previous habits"*. It values differences and it is within your Circle of Influence. It's not always "my way" or the "wrong way". There can be a third alternative that is better for everyone.

Summary of The 7 Habits of Highly Effective People: Habit 7 – Sharpen the Saw

Habit 7 *"is the habit that makes all the other habits possible"*.

Covey shares the story of a man working very hard to saw down a tree. When told it would be easier if he took a break and sharpened his saw, the man said he was too busy cutting down the tree to sharpen the saw. In life, we need to take time to **Sharpen the Saw**.

Sharpening the Saw means being proactive in taking care of your well-being. It is a **Quadrant 2 activity**,Important but Not Urgent. Therefore it is easy to put Habit 7 aside in favor or more urgent activities, until it becomes a Quadrant 1 activity, when your health fails or stress is overwhelming.

Covey maintains that in order to be successful and effective, you need to take time to **renew yourself on 4 levels**.

- **Physical** renewal includes exercise, proper nutrition and stress management.
- **Mental** renewal involves exercising the brain through reading, writing, planning and using your imagination.
- **Spiritual**renewal is value clarification, and can include prayer, study and/or meditation.
- **Social/Emotional**renewal involves service and empathy, as well as synergy and security in your relationships.

From the **physical** standpoint, we all know that exercise and healthy eating are important. When we do these things, we feel better and our stress levels are lower. It's something we should do every day, and the long-term results are incredible.

Effective exercise should include a balance of 3 components – endurance or aerobic exercise, flexibility or stretching, and strength or resistance training. Always check with a doctor regarding exercise and diet.

The **spiritual** component of Habit 7 is related to Habit 2, **Begin with the End in Mind**. This is a private part of your life and it's different for everyone. It may involve prayer or meditation, or simply awareness of your principles. At its core, it is time spent reflecting on your value system and your commitment to your values. It inspires you and lifts you to a higher level of being.

Much of the **mental** component comes from formal education. However, once you leave the classroom, it's important to continue to learn and expand your mind. There are many ways to exercise your mind including reading good literature, keeping a journal, writing, and using your imagination as you plan and organize. In addition, take advantage of training or continuing education opportunities that may arise.

The physical, spiritual and mental aspects of renewal are related to Habits 1, 2 and 3. They are *"centered on the principles of personal vision, leadership and management."* Covey recommends spending an hour every day on your physical, spiritual and mental renewal. He calls this the **Daily Private Victory**.

An hour spent on renewal can have a dramatic effect on your decisions and relationships. It can improve the effectiveness of the rest of your day. You may think you don't have the time, but you really don't have time not to take care of your well-being.

The **Social/Emotional** element of renewal is related to Habits 4, 5 and 6. It is *"centered on the principles of interpersonal leadership, empathic communication, and creative cooperation"*. You can renew your social/emotional dimensions everyday by using the Win/Win mentality combined with Empathic Listening and Synergy. These positive personal interactions bring peace of mind and a deep feeling of security.

As you work on Habit 7, Covey suggests you **try these exercises**.

- Make a list of physical activities that you enjoy that can help you keep physically fit.
- Select one of these activities and list it as a goal for the next week. Evaluate your performance at the end of the week. If you didn't accomplish your goal, ask yourself the following questions. Did you put it aside for a higher value activity? Or, did you fail to act with integrity to your values?
- Make similar lists of activities for your spiritual and mental renewal. For your social/emotional renewal, think of a few relationships you'd like to improve. Select a spiritual item, a mental activity, and a relationship. Implement a plan of renewal for

these areas. Evaluate at the end of the week.

- Every week, write down Sharpen the Saw activities for all 4 renewal areas. Commit to doing them and to evaluating your performance and the results.

Habit 7 – Renewal. Devote attention to your physical, mental, spiritual and social/emotional dimensions. These 4 renewal elements are interrelated, and improving one area strengthens the others. Similarly, ignoring an area weakens the others. *"Your physical health affects your mental health; your spiritual strength affects your social/emotional strength."* Take the time to **Sharpen the Saw**, and remember that balanced renewal gives you strength to focus on your Circle of Influence, which takes us back to the very beginning of the 7 Habits.

III.

Additional Reading

Major Reviews of The 7 Habits of Highly Effective People by Stephen Covey

Review by Tom Peters, author of "In Search of Excellence"

www.shealon.com/books.htm

"Guided by Covey's remarkable step-by-step program, readers will find more meaning and satisfaction in relationships, be better able to achieve personal and professional goals–and can look forward to lasting happiness and success. A wonderful book that could change your life."

Review by Daniel M. Wood, founder of "Looking to Business" website

lookingtobusiness.com/product-reviews/book-review-the-7-habits-of-highly-effective-people-by-stephen-covey

"Probably the most read book on personal development…. The reasons are apparent; Stephen Covey has a gift with words and a gentle way of challenging us to see the better in ourselves and to take responsibility for our actions and our lives."

Review by Warren Bennis, Distinguished Professor of Business at the University of Southern California, author of "On Becoming a Leader.

www.your-brain-at-work.com/reviews/index.shtml

"This is the best, the most helpful, and the brainiest book I've read on how the brain affects how, why and what we do and act. After reading only the first four chapters, I felt roughly 100% more efficient in organizing my work and personal life."

Review by Joan Price, author of "The Anytime, Anywhere Exercise Book"

www.sterlingspeakers.com/covey.htm

"*The 7 Habits of Highly Effective People* was a groundbreaker when it was first published in 1989, and it continues to be a business bestseller with more than 15 million copies sold. Stephen Covey, an internationally respected leadership authority, realizes that true success encompasses a balance of personal and professional effectiveness, so this book is a manual for performing better in both arenas. His anecdotes are as frequently from family situations as from business challenges."

Review by Businessballs

www.businessballs.com/sevenhabitsstevencovey.htm

"The 'Seven Habits' are a remarkable set of inspirational and aspirational standards for anyone who seeks to live a full, purposeful and good life, and are applicable today more than ever, as the business world becomes more attuned to humanist concepts. Covey's values are full of integrity and humanity, and contrast strongly with the process-based ideologies that characterized management thinking in earlier times."

Review by MindTools

www.mindtools.com/pages/article/newLDR_79.htm

"This is one of the best-known leadership books of recent years… Rather than tackling specific problems or making external changes to processes, systems and so on, Covey's approach helps you focus on developing yourself personally and your relationships with others."

Interesting Related Online Content

This article describes the differences between the personality ethic and character ethic. It then summarizes the path to interdependence: www.quickmba.com/mgmt/7hab/

This website gives a brief summary of the book and provides links to inspirational quotes and poems. It also provides a link to related reading material: www.whitedovebooks.co.uk/7-habits/7-habits.htm

The American Management Association describes a 3 day course based on the "The 7 Habits of Highly Effective People". The course outlines ways to achieve balance and increase productivity:www.amanet.org/7-Habits

This article presents an exclusive interview with Covey. It covers his daily work ethic and his views on other self-help books: zenhabits.net/exclusive-interview-stephen-covey-on-his-morning-routine-blogs-technology-gtd-and-the-secret/

This website shares some notable and inspirational quotes by Covey: www.goodreads.com/author/quotes/1538.Stephen_R_Covey

Interesting Facts Related to The 7 Habits of Highly Effective People and Stephen Covey

- Stephen Covey was born in 1932 in Salt Lake City, Utah.
- Covey's father was an apostle and counselor in the Mormon Church.
- He and his wife, Sandra, have 9 children and over 50 grandchildren.
- Covey makes an effort every morning to win what he calls the "Daily Private Victory." This includes exercising on a stationary bike while studying the Bible for at least 30 minutes. This is followed by 15 minutes of swimming and 15 minutes of water yoga.
- Covey prays daily with what he calls a listening spirit, while visualizing the rest of his day. This includes focusing on professional activities and important relationships.
- Covey averages 2 hours of reading each day.
- Covey regards modern technology as one of his weaknesses.
- Covey also finds most meetings are a waste of time because there is often little opportunity for synergy to produce better solutions.

Table of Contents

I. Quicklet on Stephen Covey's The 7 Habits of Highly Effective Families

Quicklet on Stephen Covey's The 7 Habits of Highly Effective Families

About Stephen Covey's The 7 Habits of Highly Effective Families

"I am convinced that if we as a society work diligently in every other area of life and neglect the family, it would be analogous to straightening deck chairs on the Titanic." – Dr. Covey

The 7 Habits of Highly Effective Families takes the 7 Habits he teaches in *The 7 Habits of Highly Effective People,* and applies them to the family. After many clients and others that the author knew approached him about how the 7 Habits would play in the family environment, he decided to create this book.

This edition of the 7 Habits became a *New York Times* bestseller in 1997, when it was published. According to Dr. Covey's biography, it continues to be the number one hardcover book on the family. (The 3rd Alternative Bio)

Dr. Covey shares in a personal message at the beginning of the book that it was difficult for him to decide whether or not to include all of the stories and experiences from his own family that he was considering. He battled with this because he didn't want to come across as a know-it-all, but the author also knew what had truly worked first hand for them and wanted to share that truth with the world. Much of the book has stories from his wife, including a foreward from her, and from their nine children.

Meet the Author, Stephen Covey

Via Wikimedia Commons.

Dr. Stephen R. Covey, born October 24, 1932 in Salt Lake City, Utah, received his doctorate at Brigham Young University, an MBA while at Harvard, and a bachelor's in business administration from the University of Utah. He steers clear of preaching his religion or politics in this work, but he does share some of his values.

Over 20 million of Dr. Covey's books have sold in 38 languages. He has received the International Man of Peace Award, National Fatherhood Award, and the International Entrepreneur of the Year Award. (Stephen R. Covey Community Bio)

Dr, Covey is the co-founder and vice chairman of FranklinCovey, the number one worldwide professional services firm. The doctor is not only an author, founder, and chairman, he is also a public speaker. The clients of FranklinCovey are in the the thousands, including 90% of the Fortune 100 and 75% of the Fortune 500. (FranklinCovey About Us)

He is currently a professor at the Jon M. Huntsman School of Business at Utah State University. (Utah State University)

Dr. Covey is married with nine children and is a grandfather and great-grandfather. He lives in Utah.

Overall Summary of The 7 Habits of Highly Effective Families

"There are certain fundamental principles that govern in all human interactions, and living in harmony with those principles or natural laws is absolutely essential for quality family life." – Dr. Covey

Families that are unified and strong are a great deal of work, and require each family member's participation. Each is to add their talents, energy, vision, desire, and dedication to the whole. Dr. Covey takes the 7 Habits that he taught in his work *The 7 Habits of Highly Effective People* and transposes them into the family environment, teaching these principles and showing how to apply them to real life situations, regardless of the current shape or size of one's family.

He shares personal insight from his own life, along with the experience having taught the 7 Habits for years. He is an expert on on how to repair relationships, to use games with children to accomplish unifying the family unit, along with using meetings to consult with one another on decisions. Real life experiences from Dr. Covey's own family are used to illustrate how this is done.

The book goes to great lengths to illustrate, from the point of view of many different sources who are regular people – wives, husbands, parents and grandparents – the problems that plague the family and how they used one or more of the 7 Habits to overcome those problems.

Each chapter goes into the 7 Habits, with a summarizing chapter at the end of how to get from a family that is just surviving to a family that has significance, once the reader is able to put the simple but complex principles into motion and use them over the course of years and into their lifetime to come. Teaching how to really listen, build trust, discipline, and guide children to be responsible for themselves are main themes that run throughout the work.

The guide of how to create a Family Mission Statement, similar to a mission statement that corporations create, is explained in great detail. Using time wisely to build relationships with one's significant other and each child, and keep those personal, individual relationships strong, is a key component.

The metaphor of how pilots deviate from their flight plan ninety percent of the time is used throughout the book. Due to weather, navigation around other airplanes and information from traffic control towers, pilots must change course during a flight constantly, but they always refer back to the original flight plan. The same goes for how one wants to raise their children and work with their significant other. We all desire to be in a happy family and reach the destination together, but there will be fluctuations to those plans.

Three Purposes of the Book

- **Clear Vision:** Create a family mission statement with all parties involved, so everyone knows the goal you are trying to achieve.
- **Flight Plan:** The 7 Habits framework that Covey teaches in the book.
- **Compass:** Aiding the reader in finding his or her own talents to contribute to building their family.

The miracle of the **Chinese Bamboo Tree** is used quite often. The reason is because once the seed is planted, only a tiny shoot is visible above ground for four years. The root structure is growing, though, so in the fifth year, the tree grows up to eighty feet tall. Dr. Covey uses this fun fact to show that his 7 Habits may not appear to make much impact on your family initially, and it may take months or even years for some, but eventually all of the hard work you have done will come to pass when an estranged loved one or extremely difficult problem finally comes to terms.

As a whole, this work is outstanding for anyone who is seeking to use one, a few, or all of the tools created by Dr. Covey. It's also appropriate for someone who is simply looking for a guideline on how to prioritize their family to the number one spot on their list. It is easily read, quick to understand and absorb, with tools and basic fundamentals that all mankind has and can appreciate.

Chapter One: You're Going to Be "Off Track" 90% of the Time. So What?

*"In general, I'd say that our family had as many fights as other families when we were growing up. We had our share of problems, too. But I am convinced that it was the ability to renew, to apologize, and to start again that made our family relationships strong." –
Sean Covey*

Three Purposes of The Book

- A clear vision of your destination
- A flight plan
- A compass

Pilots use a flight plan for every flight they have scheduled. However, due to weather, other planes flying in the area, information from traffic control towers, and even faulty equipment, the pilots must deviate off course much of the time – in fact, ninety percent of the time. However, this does not change the original flight plan, which they consistently refer to and return to as soon as conditions permit. This theme is used throughout the book to show how having a vision in mind with one's family is important, but it is also crucial to remember that one must remember that much that life will throw our way will interfere with our goal.

Dr. Covey explores how life has changed in the thirty years prior to when this edition of 7 Habits was published, in the 90's with crime, divorce, health problems, scholastic achievement, single family homes, teen suicide and sexually transmitted diseases have all increased.

He gives the 7 Habits and the additional tools in the book as the solution to society's ills and how to protect your family from becoming a victim to them.

The statistics Dr. Covey uses are from 1990, which are 12 years old now. Here are some of the latest statistics to give a realistic view of how the family is currently under attack.

- Births to unwed mothers totaled 1,693,658 in 2009. (Centers for Disease Control and Prevention)
- As of 2011, 50% percent of first marriages, 67% of second and 74% of third marriages end in divorce. (Divorce Updates)
- People who have been victims of stalking, physical violence and/or rape of an intimate partner as adults first experienced some kind of violence from a partner between the ages of 11 and 17. This is true for 15% for men and 22.4% of women. (Centers for Disease Control and Prevention)

Having a vision is to create a Family Mission Statement, which is developed by all members of the family. It becomes the document, or motto, that the "pilots" adhere to and refer back to, again and again, when facing adversity and conflict.

The 7 Habits framework becomes the flight plan, showing one how to reach the vision of the Family Mission Statement. The seven principles, which are delved into in detail in forthcoming chapters, give light where there is darkness to the person seeking information on how to communicate with their children, or "flight crew," in the most loving, effective ways.

The third component of this is the compass. Anyone who desires change for the better in their family will be able to have it with work, and thus they become an agent of change, or a compass, showing which way is true north at all times. Each of us are the expert on our families.

Involve your family right from the beginning of the process. Even with those who resist, inform them of what you are working towards.

Chapter Two: Habit 1 – Be Proactive

"The way you treat any relationship in the family will eventually affect every relationship in the family." – Dr. Covey

Between stimulus and response, there is a gap in time where one has the ability to use their freedom to choose how they will respond. This is what Dr. Covey translates into being proactive as opposed to reactive.

Instead of reacting to what goes on around us without any thought, it is best to be proactive, to stop and think about the situation at hand, gather information pertinent to the circumstances and then make the best choice possible, even if it is only our attitude that we are able to have a choice in.

Animals do not have the ability to make choices. Everything they do comes from instinct and survival. There are four gifts that human beings have which separate them from the animals when it comes to how we behave and live. Those four gifts are self-awareness, conscience, imagination and independent will.

By being self-aware, humans are able to observe thoughts. We have the ability to be aware of who we are, why and how we came to be that way, and we have the function to separate ourselves from what we have done to contemplate our lives.

All of us are born with a conscience, the capacity to know the difference between what is right or wrong. Now, that knowledge may dim over time due to extenuating circumstances such as abuse, drug usage or decades of criminal behavior, but it is still present. Only those who are born with a limited mental ability have a decreased conscience from the get-go.

Imagination is a gift that all mankind has, giving us the usage of envisioning life different as we know it now. This is a wonderful part of the brain where problem solving and seeing the potential of one's family may be utilized and quite useful.

The last gift, independent will, means we are free to do as we desire. We are not controlled by instinct or survival. It is the power to make things happen.

These four gifts are all part of the area of our minds where the pause button is, where we have the chance to think of how we will react to a person or situation that comes across us, instead of just reacting blindly.

Dr. Covey goes into the explanation that he believes there is another human gift, a fifth one, being a sense of humor. People must have the skill to laugh at themselves and each other. No matter how well thought out plans are made, regardless the expertise of the information brought home and presented, things will go wrong at times. We have to be able to laugh and not fall apart when mistakes are made and weaknesses are shown, because they will happen often. No one is perfect.

There is a story about a man who approaches Dr. Covey at a seminar because he didn't love his wife anymore. The author, after asking the man some questions, told him that he needed to love his wife. The man, confused, didn't understand what he was getting at. Dr. Covey explained that love is a verb, and that love – the feeling – is something that comes as a result. He goes on to say that Hollywood and the media want us to believe that love is only the feeling and it doesn't have to be worked for, but that is untrue.

Being proactive in your life means to make an effort to cultivate the relationships in your life with your actions and attitude, like a garden, not thinking that just because there were a few flourishing flowers there that they'll stay alive on their own without tending.

Dr. Covey shares that he has had thousands of people complete a questionnaire about their four unique gifts, and always, the gift that is most neglected is self-awareness. However, it is very important to elevate the family and to be self-aware of the family's identity so that it may constantly improve. The family must tend to one another, strengthen bonds and solve issues as quickly as possible.

We need to focus on the things that we are able to influence. This introduces what Covey calls the Circle of Influence and the Circle of Concern. Picture a large circle, the Circle of Concern, with a smaller circle inside of it, which is the Circle of Influence. Everything that we are worried about and want to control is in the area of Concern, while what we can actually do something about is in the area of Influence. Being proactive, one spends their energy on items within the realms of the Circle of Influence.

A paradigm is given of the Emotional Bank Account. This is to illustrate that relationships are like a checking account; as positive experiences and encouraging words are given, deposits are made, and as negative experiences occur with a family member, withdrawals occur. Consistent deposits keep a relationship in the black when someone's feelings are hurt, whereas, constant withdrawals with few deposits put a relationship in the red.

Being kind, apologizing, being loyal to those not present, making and keeping promises, and forgiving are all specific ways that deposits are made into the Emotional Bank Account. This is because they are based on the Primary Laws of Love, which are ways that unconditional love is shown. They are acceptance, understanding, and participation.

Chapter Three: Habit Two – Begin With the End in Mind

"A family mission statement is a combined, unified expression from all family members of what your family is all about and the principles you choose to govern your family life." – Dr. Covey

This chapter is about the second habit, which is having the end in your mind, your vision, of where you want to end up. Thus, for the family, it is to create the Family Mission Statement which includes the values and rules you all want to govern your lives.

Covey states this is done through the following steps:

- Explore what your family is all about
- Write your family mission statement
- Use it to stay on track

First, have meetings with everyone in your family. This will vary predicated upon if you have little children, if your family has someone who rebels and refuses to participate, etc. Explain to them you are working on a Family Mission Statement, what it is and the goal. There are multiple ways of going about gathering their input, whether doing it over a long period of a succession of meetings or after just one gathering. You are the expert on your family and you will know what works best for you.

Next, write the mission statement. It may be in a form other than a written out paragraph, such as a song, poem, one sentence or even a symbol. After everyone has had their say, and they are in agreement of where the plane of your family is headed, write it out or create it and distribute copies as needed. Post it where everyone may view it such as over the fireplace mantle, on the family room wall or to hang in each family member's bedroom.

Last, use it! Reflect on your mission statement at holidays, birthdays, and at mealtime. Are you on the right path still? What corrections need to be made? Children are fantastic at reminding parents when they are not staying in integrity to the agreed upon mission statement. It will also be a great tool for discipline when a child is acting out against the mission statement, a parent will remind them of what was agreed upon by the entire family. This will assist parents in not wanting to be friends with their children in order to win popularity contests They will remain as the pilots for their crew.

A Family Mission Statement carries its sizeable power because love is a verb. Through their daily life in the household, the family shows its love to everyone else by staying congruent to the statement and making amends when they are amiss.

This statement can also help with the extended family. There is noa reason to limit it to just parents and children. Including grandparents, uncles, aunts, cousins and so forth in a grand Family Mission Statement that all agree upon would be fantastic. It would also carry on through future generations throughout the extended family.

Dr. Covey gives three items to watch out for while creating the Family Mission Statement:

- Don't announce it
- Don't rush it
- Don't ignore it

For the first step, it is not for one person to come up with a mission statement all on their own and then tell the rest of the family "how it is." Everyone needs to be part of the planning and contribution. Otherwise it won't be respected or used. In addition, it will take time to come to statement that all parties agree to. Don't feel that you are under a deadline; take your time. Third, once the statement is complete, don't forget about it. Use it, display it and remember it as a reference point often.

You are able to create a Family Mission Statement online with your family on the FranklinCovey website at no charge.

Chapter Four: Habit Three – Put First Things First

"The place to start is not with the assumption that work is non-negotiable; it's with the assumption that family is non-negotiable. That one shift of mind-set opens the door to all kinds of creative possibilities." – Dr. Covey

This chapter is all about the third habit in the 7 Habits framework, prioritizing and putting what matters most at the top of the list. Covey introduces two designs to achieve this with the Family Mission Statement.

One is having family time, where there is a designated time each week with the family. The other is to have time just with the two of you, one-on-one.

In Covey's surveys of over a quarter of a million people, Habit 3 is the one where people give themselves the lowest marks. In reference, he quotes an article about the five lies parents tell themselves why they must work. They are:

- We need the extra money
- Day care is perfectly good
- Inflexible companies are the key problem
- Dads would gladly stay home if their wives earned more money
- High taxes force both of us to work

(US News & World Report)

People must decide that if their family truly is a top priority for them, how they are going to give up other things that detract from that priority, even if it is a second income, hobbies, or luxuries that give momentary pleasure but cause long-term harm. Being a parent is one of the paramount roles in life, second to being a spouse. Daycare is needed by many, and when a parent is to hire outside services to raise their child, a thorough, careful, well informed decision needs to be made before choosing who is going to be stepping into that role for them while they are away.

For many, the place of employment has become the place of relaxation as well as refuge from life, when in years past, it was the home that was the provider for these needs. Many businesses give their employees perks, benefits and rewards to burn the midnight oil, never a reason to leave to venture back home. They have the convenience of food, employee lounges, showers, gyms and much more to give them all the comforts they would have where they live. Many people spend their free time with their colleagues instead of their families and have completely different social lives and circles separate from each other. A haven is created by the employer for people to revel in and enjoy, so they do not need to go home to the angry spouse or empty apartment.

However, when one is an outstanding parent, the awards are all emotional and intangible. Children do not sign paychecks for their mother for all the housework she's done and for helping them with homework. Dads are not praised with free drinks and an extra day of vacation for completing the add on to the basement. The payback of being a good, strong parent comes from the heart, and being proactive, one must seek this payback instead of the phony, short lived kind tossed out in the workplace.

Raising a family today in a society who does not sustain a family, with an economy that wants to tear family apart, and the law which has unraveled, creates an environment where there is not a safety net, as Dr. Covey states. To use the airplane metaphor again, we experience vertigo because we aren't able to feel what is going on around us without the use of the tools and instruments at our fingertips as pilots.

The metaphor of the compass is something Dr. Covey uses throughout his travels as a worldwide speaker. He brings out a compass and shows the audience the north indicator and explains how that doesn't change. He then goes through the following points:

- Just as there is a true north, so there are natural laws or principles that never change
- There is a difference between principles and our behavior
- There is a difference between natural systems and social systems

- The essence of real happiness and success is to align the direction of travel with natural laws or principles
- It's possible for our deep, inward sense of knowing to become changed, subordinated, even eclipsed by traditions or by repeated violation of one's own conscience

Turn your mission statement into reality with weekly family time. However you have family time, whether it be through games, having a dinner where everyone is present, going out to a show, or whatever you think of to spend quality time together, the point of weekly family time is to meet some basic needs that people have, which are to have fun by being social, mental by teaching, physical by solving problems and spiritual by planning and/or worshipping.

Image via Wikimedia Commons.

Having one-on-one time with your spouse and then also with each child is also vital to a happy family. Again, how you spend your time varies. Suggestions are to plan with your spouse the financial goals or dreams for the upcoming year, discuss problems, address issues in your marriage, enjoy each other's company and have fun. With children, each parent is to spend time alone with each child on a regular basis, preferably weekly. You and your child may decide they get to always choose the activity or you may take turns. Take the time to teach them skills they need at the appropriate age and time they are experiencing life, play with them or simply talk. Money spent on them, spouse or child, will not be remembered and is not the important component of this exercise. It is the building up of the relationship, putting deposits in the emotional bank account, gaining trust and seeking to understand one another.

Chapter Five: Habit Four - Think "Win-Win"

"The principle is this: What is important to another person must be as important to you as the other person is to you." – Dr. Covey

Image via Wikimedia Commons.

Otherwise known as the Golden Rule, to do unto others as they would do unto you, the fourth habit in the series seeks to have both parties win.

Those who only want a win-lose environment for their family members seeks to control them and force their will upon them, and definitely don't seek to understand them or take the time to envision the end result. The consequences of a win-lose home mean that it is pitting one ego against another, one believes he is always right, and it alienates family members from the dominant ego.

A lose-win position means that one is constantly stepped on, their needs not being met and it may even lead to the detriment of their very being and self-esteem. If someone is never able to win or be acknowledged for their efforts, ideas, feelings and opinions, it can breed co-dependency, depression, or ultimately suicide.

Win-win is the only alternative that is long-term to a win-lose or lose-win possibility. Basically, what someone believes to be important to them, needs to be important to you. With unconditional love, you are able to take the time and steps necessary to ensure a win-win when conflicts come up and decisions are to be made.

To have a **scarcity mentality** is to think that if someone wins or receives more than you, there is less for you to have and win. An **abundance mentality** is that there is enough for all to win.

How Dr. Covey explains how to use the win-win concept with children:

- You can let them win in the little things
- You can interact with them around the big things
- You can take steps to offset the competition focus
- Create a win-win agreement

In the trivial items of the day, such as a three year old wanting to wear mismatched clothing, let the child have their way. This puts a deposit in your account from the view of the child. When it comes to weightier matters, discussing with your teenager their ideas for solving a problem with carpooling the kids to school is beneficial because it builds trust and communication, and they may also give additional insight and solutions that you wouldn't have come up with alone. Assist your children when they want to compete against each other, their friends or competitors when playing sports to see the bigger picture or help them to coach each other.

Creating a written win-win agreement to resolve issues is another step in the right direction for strengthening your family and helping your children become self-reliant and responsible adults. It is a great tool for teaching them how to be stewards over their chores, overcome mistakes and achieve common goals.

The five elements of a win-win agreement are:

- Desired results
- Guidelines
- Resources
- Accountability
- Consequences

Explain the results you want, what the guidelines are to obtain them, what resources are available to your child to work on the chore, problem, etc., and how they are to report the success of their work. Then review the consequences, good and bad, of what happens should the agreement be upheld or if it is not. Then, when a child is given the opportunity to govern themselves, they will do so. When faced with accountability of their actions, according to what they have sown, they will reap the corresponding consequences. They won't have an argument against that, as they will have been told up front all of the pertinent information in the agreement which they signed to, either literally or figuratively.

The main key to win-win is to look at the big picture. Looking at misbehavior with a temporary solution without keeping in mind that the child will one day grow to be an adult in our society is definitely not looking at the problem with the end in mind. Giving discipline that a child can understand with an attitude of reminding them of what the Family Mission Statement is and how their behavior was not congruent with it is a win-win alternative to telling them no TV for a day.

Chapter Six: Habit Five – Seek First to Understand…Then to be Understood

"Two major problems in communication are perception, or how people interpret the same data, and semantics, or how people define the same word. Through empathic understanding, both of these problems can be overcome." – Dr. Covey

Dr. Covey states that people do not see the world as it is, they see it as they are, or as they have been conditioned to be.

He demonstrates this by sharing an object lesson he uses while lecturing. He asks for a volunteer to give him their eyeglasses, asks another volunteer to wear them. He then uses various tactics from cajoling to force to insult to convince the person wearing a stranger's prescription glasses that they can see clearly what is before them.

Many misunderstandings in life occur because we believe that we know exactly what the problem is and what the solution is. Yet, in reality, we do not have all of the facts and the solution is something completely different than we thought. Perhaps it's not even within the same realm of possibility, because the other party involved is seeing the experience in a way we can not.

This comes into play especially with small children who lack the judgment and understanding of what is going on, along with limited language to explain to us what they perceive and feel. The adults must take the time to find out what the child sees to know all facts and information involved in order to help them and make the appropriate action.

Wanting to understand is one of the highest forms of deposit into the Emotional Bank Account. Judging people and being predjudiced stems from the lazy route of wanting to protect oneself and not taking the time to get to know and understand someone.

People also need room to breathe, or psychological air, meaning they need to get out their feelings that are building inside of them in a safe environment. Until someone receives this, the need to be understood keeps building up, more and more. Eventually they will explode, which is why people yell at each other. They are starved for understanding. Taking the time to understand someone when the signs that something is wrong right at the start will give that person the psychological air they need to vent and be able to move on, even if circumstances do not allow a solution to the problem at hand for the time being.

You aren't able to give a real deposit into a person's Emotional Bank Account if you don't know them and know what matters to them. Each of us have different ways of showing and receiving love, and what one man may deem to be of great worth, another may view as trivial. Your child may relish time spent with them over anything else, while your wife enjoys time spent with her, but it's when you show her with affection that the deposits skyrocket.

"Creating a warm, caring, supportive, encouraging environment is probably the most important thing you can do for your family," Dr. Covey states.

Putting away sensitivities avoid being offended and angry over nothing is essential to this habit. Almost always, the person that hurt us didn't intend to do so, and getting offended is a choice. Also, when anger is used to be out of control, it sets the rest of the family on edge. Trust can not be built in this enviornment. Vulnerability will not be present at all.

In order to overcome hurt feelings and negativity, they must be talked through and understood. Show your vulnerability and in turn, the other family member will feel safe to be vulnerable. Forgiveness comes about more easily when both people involved process what happened together. Humility is a part of this and with it comes greater, firmer bonds.

Empathic listening is the highest form of listening, better than doling out advice or judgments or selectively hearing what is being said. It requires discipline and empathy on the part of the hearer, with the ability to repeat back to the listener what was said – not necessarily verbatim, but with the meaning behind the words.

The principles behind empathic listening are to repeat back to your loved one what you are hearing them say as they share their feelings instead of telling them what they should feel. It requires a true, real desire to understand them, not judge them or give unwanted advice.

To seek to be understood, one shares what they know, teaches their children, gives feedback – including helpful criticism, and tells others their opinions, advice and so forth. They don't hide their light and knowledge.

Dr. Covey suggests the following when you need to confront someone:

- Always ask yourself if the feedback will really help them or if you just want to fill your need to be right. Wanting to truly help someone as opposed to seeking your own agenda in anger is night and day.
- Seek first to understand. Find out why they did what they did, the circumstances surrounding it, their feelings about it and what else is going on in their lives that could have attributed to the problem.
- Separate the person from the behavior. Remember to love your family unconditionally. It is the behavior that is unacceptable, not the person.
- Be especially sensitive and patient to blind spots. If someone is clueless about something they've done wrong, what would be the point of confronting them? Consider perception, age of a child, and whether someone is in denial of their blind spot. People won't be receptive to criticism about something that don't see as a problem.
- Use "I" messages. Explain how the behavior affected you, by saying, "I was hurt when you did that." Do not attack with "you" messages, such as, "You were a complete jerk when you said it." Share how you feel about what happened and how you saw it. Otherwise, you send the message to the person that you know all and have labeled them and their actions as less than yourself.

To cultivate a Habit 5 environment, your family needs to practice till they reach the point where they can sit down and hear each other out through empathic listening when there is a problem. The first person must listen to the second person and repeat to them what they are saying, until the second person says the first does understand them, before the first person may begin to explain their position. This is how real empathic listening can come into play and break down heated situations into win-win partnerships.

Also, in order to apply Habit 5, one has to understand the stages that children go through in development. There are certain developmental stages that all babies and children participate in as they age, and in order to properly parent them, we have to learn what those are and when they occur.

Dr. Covey shares the following questions to consider before having a child take on a task:

- Should the child do it
- Can the child do it

- Does the child want to do it

Questioning if the child should do it stems from one's value system; is it something safe and appropriate for that child to handle, given their age, maturity, level of understanding, past experiences, etc.? Considering if a child can do it is to measure their competency. Wondering whether the child wants to do it or not stems from motivation. They meet the first two criteria, but there has to be an addition to the equation if motivation is a problem, such as a reward from the outside like an allowance or helping them to see that an inward prize of self-pride and satisfaction will be fulfilling. Both options as well could be used too.

Chapter Seven: Habit Six – Synergize

"You must be able to say sincerely, 'The fact that we see things differently is a strength – not a weakness – in our relationship.'" – Dr. Covey

To synergize means to cooperate with others. This sixth habit in the series of the 7 Habits is what Dr. Covey refers to as the **summmum bonum**, or supreme or highest fruit, of all the habits. Synergizing as a family is when all members come together to work collectively as one.

Being able to see the differences in one another and appreciate them as beautiful and creating a whole is a miracle. It's an adventure, full of risk, and well worth taking. Men and women have basic fundamental differences from the start. They are able to get past those differences and celebrate them in the creation of a child. Why stop there?

Many marriages start out with admiration and then it turns to irritation when they see the differences. Turn this around in your life. See how the strengths of your partner make up for your weaknesses. Realize that a talent you possess is nourished by a talent your husband has and find a way to use them to bond and work together. Reconcile differences in how to run the household, raise children, budget and everything else by working together with a willingness to create something bigger than the two of you could ever accomplish alone.

Through the practice of the 7 Habits, your unit will create its own Family Immune System. When there is a sudden death in the family, illness strikes, a financial upheaval or other attack on your family, it won't destroy it or even come close because with the synergy of using the habits on a regular basis, which is the Family Immune System, it will buffer any blows that come in and make them much easier to handle.

A Synergy Exercise

Take an issue that needs to be resolved and go through the following steps with your family. Going through the process with show how everyone may have a hand in finding a solution and working together.

- What is the problem from everyone's point of view?
- What are the key issues involved?
- What would constitute a fully acceptable solution?
- What new options would meet that criteria?

In another form of synergy, called transactional plus synergy, the cooperation of two people instead of creating something new is the essence of the relationship. This takes a lot of self-awareness.

Not all circumstances require synergy, however. If there is a minor issue at hand where some feel quite strongly about the decision whereas the rest of the family doesn't, then going with those who feel strongly makes sense. Asking on a scale of one to ten how your family feels on such matters is how Dr. Covey's family resolves this issue. An example would be having a carload of kids with some wanting to go play at the park while one wants to go to the beach but says she feels so at a 2.

Remember that this process will take time. Having synergy with a spouse and with one's children takes effort on everyone's part. Reflecting back to the Chinese Bamboo Tree, it may take years before synergy takes place, but the roots will be growing and taking shape, with rare exception.

Synergy sends the message to your loved ones that regardless of how long it takes, you will make the time to understand them, to work with them, and love them unconditionally.

Chapter Eight: Habit Seven – Sharpen the Saw

"Sharpening the saw is the single highest leverage activity in life because it affects everything else so powerfully." – Dr. Covey

Entropy will set in on the relationships you have in your family if you don't sharpen the saw – that is, keep the plane well fueled, maintained and cleaned.

Image via Wikimedia Commons.

The analogy with the saw goes like this: You are a lumberjack, sawing away at a tree, and you see that another lumberjack is sawing through his tree at double the pace you are. When you inquire what his secret is, he tells you that he is taking the time between sawing to sharpen the saw.

The Emotional Bank Accounts need to have regular deposits made. Families can sharpen the saw by increasing their mental, physical, spiritual, and emotional capabilities. Continuing education, exercising together, attending church regularly, and give service are some of the ways that this may be done.

There are also other ways to sharpen the saw, such as through traditions. The following are examples by Dr. Covey:

- Family dinners
- Family vacations
- Birthdays
- Holidays
- Extended family activities
- Learning together
- Worshiping together
- Working together
- Serving together
- Having fun together

Traditions bring regeneration and an atmosphere of joy. In this spirit, people who are not relatives can be embraced into the family, such as friends or neighbors, and inducted into the family tradition. It gives a sense of hope and friendship to many who do not have it in their own home, and it sparks the beginning of them bringing the same values into their own families.

Chapter Nine: From Survival...to Stability...to Success...to Significance

"There are many ways to become involved in significance – within the family, with other families, and in society as a whole." – Dr. Covey

There are four levels of a family which shows their success rate, namely:

- Survival – When the basic human needs of clothing, food, and shelter are all that a family can focus on, a family is at the survival level. They are not able to get past this part of their lives to create anything better until these basic needs are met.
- Stability – The basic needs are being met, but home is still just a building and relationships are not cultivated or thought of. The focus point of the family is to work to provide for their needs and wants and not much else. They are dissatisfied with the situation but unable or unwilling to look for a higher way of living.
- Success – Their family is a huge part of their lives. They set goals and achieve them. The family has happiness and success with one another, but something is still missing.
- Significance – The family has found an outward calling, where they are able to serve the world and help build it up in whatever way(s) it is able to do so with the strengths and resources that it possesses. A contribution to the family of society uplifts the family to greater heights.

In order to get to the significance level, get rid of the restraining forces and build on the proactive, driving forces to bring you there.

Dr. Covey gives the Principle-Centered Family Leadership Tree as a guide for how to move towards the signfigance tier.

- Modeling – Children learn by example. Parents need to act the way they want their children to act. It's that simple. It's impossible to not model for your children. They see everything you do, whether consciously or unconsciously.

- Mentoring – Building the Emotional Bank Accounts, showing your family that you care and are sincere in your efforts to help them grow and mature. Then your advice won't fall on deaf ears.
- Organizing – Putting into action what your promises stated. Create structures that will put into practice the principles in your Family Mission Statement and uphold them. Make sure that Family Time is held each week. Don't cancel on your one-on-ones and have a plan for what you are going to do with them.
- Teaching – A parent's role as a teacher can not be replaced. Tutor your children in their schoolwork. Teach them how to care for themselves. Be there to guide them and show them the way. What is taught will come from the mission statement too.

As you strive to do all of these things, keep in mind that you do them already as a parent. Also, remember that you are a leader. Someone who models, mentors, organizes and teaches is a leader and a force. What you may need to change is how you go about fulfilling these roles and doing them better.

Three Common Mistakes in Regards to the Principle-Centered Family Leadership Tree:

- To think that any one role is sufficient
- To ignore the sequence
- To think that once is enough

All roles are important and need equal attention and work. It is incorrect to believe that one can jump to teaching without having a relationship of trust. It is erroneous to think that these roles are one time events, not lifetime responsibilities.

Airplanes and boats have a small surface called the **trim tab**. It is used to move a larger surface that acts as the rudder and affects the direction of the craft. A person can be the trim tab in their family to stop generations of shame, abuse, neglect, drugs and more from being carried forward.

Image via

Begin to apply the 7 Habits to your family. Use courage and love to start the process.

Dr. Covey concludes with the story of watching a TV program where two prison inmates told viewers that they did not care about anyone or anything. Then they became involved in a genealogy program to discover their ancestors, and they both found an anchor for healing. The prisoners expressed, with feeling, that they desired to share a history for their descendants to be able to understand them.

Coming home is something all human beings desire, no matter their station in life. It is an obtainable goal for all.

Key Terms & Definitions

Beautiful Family Culture: A family environment which is nurturing, everyone sincerely and truly loves being with one another, have a common belief system, and interact with life principles that really work. It is a "we" culture, not a "me" culture.

Pause Button: Stopping to think when there is a stimulus that comes towards us before we give our response, in order to choose how we will respond, ultimately in a postive and proactive fashion.

7 Habits: The 7 Habits framework that Dr. Covey invented that teach the principles for a successful, happy individual.

Be Proactive: The first habit in the 7 Habits. It means that one has free agency, an option to choose attitude, response and action in all things.

Transition Person: A person in a family that stops the passing on of bad habits, prejudices, and so on to the next generation.

Circle of Concern: Everything that one is worried about in life.

Circle of Influence: The area of your life that you actually can influence and have some control over. Inside the Circle of Concern.

Emotional Bank Account: Relationships are like bank accounts. Positive experiences and support are deposits into the account, while violations of trust and cruel words are examples of withdrawals.

Primary Laws of Love: Acceptance, understanding and participation.

Begin With the End in Mind: Habit Two of the 7 Habits, looking forward to the end result, now.

Put First Things First: Habit Three of the 7 Habits, prioritizing what is most important.

Metaphor of the Compass: A metaphor that is used to illustrate how we all know what is right and wrong and how to focus on true north to reach our goals.

Weekly Family Time: Time set aside each week to spend with your family to increase family relationships and build on basic human needs such as social and mental.

Think "Win-Win:" Habit Four of the 7 Habits, to have the person you are working with and yourself both win in the situation instead of a "win-lose" or "lose-win."

Scarcity Mentality: The belief that there is not enough of a good thing for all to win.

Abundance Mentality: The belief where everyone has the position to win, because there is enough for all.

Win-Win Agreement: A written contract by two family members to outline desired results, guidelines, resources, accountability and consequences.

Seek First to Understand…Then to be Understood: The fifth habit. Take the time to look at another's perception and information about the setting before explaining your point of view and looking for a solution.

Psychological Air: Being understood is as important as having oxygen to breathe when someone is at the point that nothing else matters.

Empathic Listening: To listen with empathy, paying attention to the body language and voice influctuation as well as what is being said, in order to completely understand.

Synergize: Habit 6, the *summum bonum* - supreme fruit – of all the habits, the sum of the parts.

Family Immune System: The synergy of using the 7 Habits habitually in a family will create a family immune system to keep it safe from outside attacks.

Transactional Plus Synergy. When the cooperation of two people is the essence of the relationship, not the creation of something new.

Sharpen the Saw: Habit 7, maintainance of the relationships and skills learned.

Trim Tab: It is a small surface on ships and aircraft used to move a larger surface that acts as the rudder, which then affects the direction of the machine.

Interesting Related Facts

- Dr. Stephen Covey has fifty-one grandchildren and two great-grandchildren.
- In 1997, Dr. Covey's business The Covey Leadership Center merged with Franklin Quest to create FranklinCovey.
- Dr. Covey is the recipient of eight honorary doctorate degrees.
- Other books that the author has published include The 7 Habits of Highly Effective People, The 8th Habit, First Things First and Principle-Centered Leadership.
- There are many stories used in this book from Dr. Covey's own family to illustrate points more elaborately from his wife and nine children, namely Sandra his spouse, then Catherine, Colleen, Cynthia, David, Jenny, Joshua, Maria, Sean, and Stephen.
- At the end of each chapter, there is a list of ideas for how to share the ideas in that chapter with the adults and teenagers in your family, followed by a separate list to do the same but in ways that the young children will understand and appreciate.
- CENGAGE Learning is a center that teaches perception using pictures to illustrate how two people can be looking at the same image but see two completely different things.
- One of the people that Dr. Covey quotes in this work was the current president of The Church of Jesus Christ of Latter-day Saints, Gordon B. Hinckley.

Sources & Additional Reading

- *New York Times*, 7 Habits of Highly Effective Families on Bestseller List
- *The 3rd Alternative*, 7 Habits of Highly Effective Families Number One Hardcover on Family
- *Stephen R. Covey Community*, Bio
- *FranklinCovey*, About Us
- *Utah State University*, Professor Stephen Covey
- *FranklinCovey*, Build a Mission Statement
- *US News & World Report*, Lies Parents Tell Themselves About Why They Work
- *Centers for Disease Control and Prevention*, Unmarried Childrearing in the United States
- *Divorce Updates*, Divorce Statistics in America
- *Centers for Disease Control and Prevention*, Understanding Teen Dating Violence
- *Parents*, Fun Family Traditions to Start Today
- *Buzzle.com*, Chinese Bamboo Tree Facts and Care
- *FHELessons.com*, Family Home Evening Ideas
- *FranklinCovey Blog*, Creating a Win-Win With Your Child
- *Dummies.com*, Win-Win Negotiating
- *Babycenter.com*, How to Find Good Daycare

Table of Contents

I. Quicklet on Stephen Covey's First Things First

Quicklet on Stephen Covey's First Things First

About the Book

"While we do control our choice of action, we cannot control the consequences of our choices. Universal laws or principles do. This means we are not in control of our lives, principles are. This idea provides key insight into the frustration people have had with the traditional time management approach to life."

First Things First by Stephen R Covey is New York Times Bestseller time management guide developed using Covey's principles of value-driven decision making originally set forth in the blockbuster *The Seven Habits of Highly Effective People*. The title of the book comes from the summary of the third habit, Keep First Things First, that is, make sure the most important things in your life are actually your highest priority.

In the introduction, Covey describes the genesis of *First Things First* in this way: "through our work at the Covey Leadership Center, we've been in contact with many people from around the world and we're constantly impressed with what they represent. They're active, hard-working, competent, caring people dedicated to making a difference. Yet these people consistently tell us of the tremendous struggle they face daily while trying to put first things first in their lives."

Covey goes on to explain the Covey Leadership Center team saw the need for a book that would provide practical, well structured advice on how to apply the Third Habit in daily life. Most time management books up until this point emphasized increasingly complex structures for getting more things done. However, these structures often only increased frustration and guilt because they didn't provide any fundamental framework for differentiating between good activities and best activities.

First Things First was originally published in 1996. It is no longer in print in hardback, and has not been updated since its initial publication. Despite this, and despite its lack of publicity in the advent of the electronic age, it still the best selling time management book of all time.

About the Author

Putting first things first is an issue at the very heart of life.

Stephen R Covey has an MBA from Harvard, a doctorate from Brigham Young University and has sold more than 20 million books in 38 different languages. He is best known for his book *The Seven Habits of Highly Effective People* which has received numerous awards and is also the best selling nonfiction audio book in history. He is also the cofounder and vice chairman of Franklin Covey Company.

The Seven Habits of Highly Effective People has spawned an entire industry of offshoot books and products. Related books include *The Seven Habits of Highly Effective Families* and *The Seven Habits of Highly Effective People Personal Workbook* as well as the *The 7 Habits of Happy Kids*, and *The Seven Habits of Highly Effective Teen*s, both authored by Sean Covey, Stephen Covey's son. Related products include various various planning calendars, time management software and an entire coaching staff dedicated to consulting according to the principles set forth in the *Seven Habits.*

According to his website, Covey's latest book, *The Eighth Habit*, has sold nearly 400,000 copies. Covey has nine children, 52 grandchildren and two great-grandchildren.

An Overall Summary

More than evolution, we need a revolution. We need to move beyond time management to life leadership.

If our society is addicted to urgency, Covey's time and life management system is the twelve step program for recovery. While other time management books emphasize working harder and smarter, *First Things First* is about working more in tune with your own sense of values because working harder and smarter at something you don't actually care about is a recipe for both frustration and disappointment.

Using the metaphor of the clock (linear task driven activities) versus the compass (value driven activities), Covey introduces the idea that perhaps maybe we should think about why we're doing what we're doing instead of trying to cram one more thing into one more exhausted day.

The heart of the structure of compass-based time management and decision making is Covey's Quadrant System which you can use to divide all your activities into relative importance and urgency. Some activities are both urgent and important, those are assigned Quadrant I. Some activities are important, but not urgent, those are assigned to Quadrant II. Other activities are urgent but not important, those are assigned Quadrant III. The items that are neither urgent nor important fall into Quadrant IV. If you want your life not to suck, says Covey, figure out what goes in Quadrant II and make it a priority.

Quadrant recognition alone could be life-changing, but *First Things First* has more to offer. Covey also beats the synergy drum so loudly and consistently that you're forced to at least think about the concept, even if it's not easy to apply in your life. Synergy, as Covey defines it, is a way of looking at both your goals and your roles. If you're trying to achieve synergy, you looking for ways in which your different roles can work together in collaboration rather than in competition. This calls for some creativity in the application (how can a being a good mom make you a good employee as well) but applied skillfully could certainly also be life changing.

Covey's concept of all human interaction as potentially collaborative (what he calls the interdependent paradigm) is a challenging concept as well, but you can actually have some fun in experimenting with its application. What if we walked through one day thinking of the world as a collective experience, every person we meet a potential collaborator, thinking that everyone is working towards the same goal? We'd have to pretend a lot, of course.

Image Via Flickr

For example, the exhausted barista at your local coffee shop might have the goal of getting you to go away as soon as possible with a minimum effort and your goal might be to get your coffee exactly as you'd like it. However, if you pretend that you have the same goal, you might be more inclined to remember that both of you have the same overarching objective, which is to survive the day and return home to the people who love you. Even if you don't keep so much as a keep paper calendar and a to-do list on a post-it and so can't really apply the interdependent paradigm to time management, looking at the world through collaborative eyes is going to make your day a little bit nicer.

Despite the potential for presenting life changing information in a way people can generally understand *First Things First* is not without controversy. In the business world, Covey's insistence that individuals are responsible for their own fate has drawn criticism for implying that employees are responsible for what are actually limitations of management. And it's true that Covey is not afraid to bring up what he calls moral absolutes. It's also true that Covey believes that these moral absolutes are revealed through what he somewhat euphemistically calls "wisdom literature," by which he means the books of the world's great religions.

The twelve step model of addiction recovery urges members to "take [from twelve step meetings] what you want and leave the rest" and perhaps that same advice is in order here. It might help to have Covey's worldview to apply the principles of value driven time management, but it's in no way essential to be religious in order to benefit from *First Things First.*

Chapter-by-Chapter Summary and Analysis

The Clock And The Compass

For many of us, there's a gap between the compass and the clock-between what's deeply important to us and how we spend our time. And this gap is not closed by traditional time management approach of doing more things faster. In fact, many of us find that increasing our speed only makes things worse.

In **How Many People On Their Deathbed Wish They'd Spent More Time At The Office** we're introduced to the guiding concept of *First Things First*,: the difference between making daily decisions based on **the clock** versus making daily decisions based on **the compass.**

The clock, Covey explains, represents what we do and how we manage our time. Things like schedules, goals, meetings, items that generally get written on to-do lists: that's what *First Things First* calls "clock" items.

The compass, in contrast, represents basic values and personally held principles, belief in what your mission is and what Covey calls conscience, or a set of internally held, absolute values. Basic right and wrong.

Much of the difficulty and angst in modern life, Covey asserts, is a result of making daily life decisions based on clock items when we should be making daily life decisions based on compass guidelines. Those feelings at the end of a long day, wondering "I did all the stuff on my to do list, but I can't believe that's all there is" is a problem of clock versus compass orientation.

It's an emphasis on the clock rather than the compass that limits the usefulness of most time management systems. The author explore the limits of these systems using the model of three generations of time management.

People using first generation concepts of time management merely write down (often called "capture") everything they need to do. First generation time management tools are all about checklists and not too much more.

Second generation time management thinking is slightly more sophisticated, and involves more emphasis on planning and preparation. Think schedules and calendars rather than a to-do list on a post-it. Third generation time management is slightly more values driven, because there is an emphasis on both planning and prioritization, but it still focuses more on the clock than the compass.

The problem with all these ways of dealing with time management is they might help people become more productive and gets lots of tasks done, but these tasks may or may not benefit what any individual counts as most important. What Covey proposes is a way of managing time that is completely governed by personal values. In the simplest terms, it is a to-do list with a conscience.

In **The Urgency Addiction** Covey explores our collective societal obsession with activities that are seen as urgent. It's counterintuitive that most time management systems fail to help us accomplish the things that are most important to us, since it seems like we would naturally choose tasks that are important merely because they are important. Covey use the addiction model to explain why this doesn't happen naturally. Because of **urgency addiction,** we choose things that are urgent, which squeezes out things that are important.

Here Covey explains the Quadrant system for dividing up tasks, with the idea that if you know what tasks are urgent and what tasks are important (or a combination of both) it simplifies value driven planning. The four quadrants are:

Quadrant I activities are things that are important and urgent, that is driven by both the clock and the compass. Examples of Quadrant I activities include deadline-driven projects, real crises, and pressing problems. The key to understanding this quadrant is that activities aren't considered Quadrant I just because they are urgent to someone else. The activities have to be important in terms of greater values.

Quadrant II activities are tasks that are important but not urgent, that is, driven by the compass and not the clock. Examples of Quadrant II activities include long range planning, preparation and activities that build relationships and community.

-**Quadrant III activities** are not important but are urgent that is, driven completely by clock and not at all by the compass. Examples of Quadrant II activities include interruptions and dealing with other people's emergencies.

-**Quadrant IV activities** are not important and not urgent, that is, driven by neither the compass nor the clock. Examples of these type of activities include, busywork, unneeded paperwork and escape activities such as watching reality television.

In order to really feel some kind of basic satisfaction with life, Covey states, people need to attend more to Quadrant II activities. However, there is a natural human tendency to mood manage with Quadrant III activities. This natural human tendency is reinforced by the pace of modern life. Managing a crisis or attending to some perceived emergency gives a hit of adrenaline that is satisfying short term and also temporarily distracts from negative emotions like boredom or existential sadness.

To illustrate this situation: imagine Sam, a pretty regular guy, walking to an appointment, plagued by thoughts of "where is my life going." Sam encounters a mugger who demands his wallet and cell phone. In the process of negotiating with the mugger or running away from the mugger, Sam stops questioning the meaning of his existence and focuses merely on doing whatever it takes to ensure that he stays safe. Focusing on Quadrant III activities is like creating a virtual mugger in order to keep us in constant emergency mode and focused away from other emotional states.

In the extremely alliteratively entitled **To Live, To Love, To Learn, To Leave A Legacy**

a system is set forth to help clarify your own values so that you can effectively use the value driven time management system described in the rest of the book. In the most practical of terms, you can't determine what's in Quadrant II if you don't really have an idea of what's truly important.

The first concept to understand in the values clarification process is what Covey calls the the fulfillment of the four human needs and capacities. The four needs are broken down into the separate categories of physical (to live), social (to love), mental (to learn) and spiritual (to leave a legacy). However, one of the concepts that makes *First Things First* unique amongst time management books is its application of the idea of **synergy** to meeting human needs.

Although synergy has become a business buzzword in the decades after *First Things First* was published, the idea of synergy as it's used here is intersection. Covey believes that meeting our four human needs through our activities isn't about a balancing act where we're juggling four balls and trying not to drop any one. Instead, the best moments in life are created when actions we take to meet one need also enable us to meet other needs.

Image via Flickr

For example, let's take the fictional example of Sam, a young single guy who lives in a big city (hence the previous mugging reference) away from his extended family and hasn't established a nuclear family yet. He needs knee surgery and won't be able to get his own groceries afterwards. He asks a neighbor for help; this meets both his social needs and his physical needs. Especially if he is able to reciprocate and help his neighbor with dog-sitting when his knee is healed, Sam has also met a spiritual need to leave a legacy by creating a sense of community and real connection in his big city apartment building. Sam has used to the concept of synergy to meet multiple needs with an activity.

The second guideline Covey gives for the values clarification process is that there are certain **true north** principles, that is ultimate principles of non-relative right or wrong. This could become a diatribe against situational ethics, but Covey doesn't go into much detail here. The main example given is the **rule of the farm.** The rule of the farm is not as much a moral absolute as it is simple cause and effect. You can't grow what you don't plant, and if you wait too long to plant it, it won't grow anyway. In other words, there are real life consequences for putting things off until the last minute.

The final guideline given to help with value clarification is to develop the four human endowments. The four human endowments are traits that Covey believes separates humans from other species : self-awareness, conscience, independent will, and creative imagination.

The Main Thing Is To Keep the Main Thing the Main Thing

This process enables you to translate your personal mission statement into the fabric of your daily life. From the mission to the moment, it empowers you to live with integrity and put first things first in a balanced, principle-centered way.

In **Quadrant II Organizing: The Process Of Putting First Things First** Covey shares the basic tools that you can use to go from clock-based time management to compass-based time management, hopefully using some of information you gathered during the values clarification process of the previous section.

The first step is to Identify your major roles. These are not necessarily the simplest roles you might assume on a daily basis, which are often closer to responsibilities. For example, if you do all the shredding of outdated paperwork at your office, that job itself is probably not really a role.

Image via Flickr

Instead, look through the overall concept of your job and see patterns of your major responsibilities. If you're supposed to do all the paperwork shredding, make sure people change their computer passcodes on a regular basis, check the smoke and carbon monoxide alarms, as well as make sure all doors are locked at the end of the day this might seem like an unrelated sets of tasks. In actuality, your role might be might defined as safety and security. Just defining your roles in this way can be a helpful clarification process, especially in workplaces with little infrastructure where everyone does everything.

Your personal roles are often more obvious. Depending on your family and social situation they might include dad, mom, friend, uncle, community builder and so on.

The second step in Quadrant II organizing is to use these main important roles to create one of two goals that are important, but not urgent and then schedule these into a weekly calendar. For example, if one of your roles is "father" and one of your goals is "spend more time talking with my son" you might schedule time to drive your son to school one morning a week in order to achieve that goal.

Making these Quadrant II (important not urgent) scheduled activities helps tame the urgency tyrant. The urgent but not important activities are forced to fit into your life around the urgent not important activities, instead of the other way around.

In **The Passion Of Vision** Covey presents a general discussion of **mission statements**, although the full process of creating a mission statement is covered in an appendix. The most important concepts about mission statements include:

-People need mission statements in order to develop long term vision that will help us make better decisions about how we spend our time.

-Lack of long term vision leads to habits like watching a lot of television which for most people is Quadrant IV activity. These kind of habits eat up time without much resulting benefit.

-Long term vision nurtures overall passion and also passion in daily life. Passion can be a vital motivating force.

Covey suggests that in order to develop a mission statement, you should consider your primary roles and who they impact most. What do you want those people to say about you about how you have fulfilled your role in their lifetime? Those desired outcomes, or **tribute statements** as Covey calls them, are the framework for a basic mission statement.

In **The Balance Of Roles**, Covey re-introduces the concept of synergy and explains some practical applications for synergy and its tenets.

The difficulty in juggling and in fact one of the reasons many people search for time management tools and solutions is the overwhelming feeling created by what *First Things First* calls the either/or complex. We struggle with choosing between what is better and what is best. Covey's solution is to focus most on developing activities that help you fulfil multiple goals.

For example, if one of your roles is "community volunteer" and one of your roles is "friend" and you feel like you don't have sufficient time to fulfill both roles, what can you do? Outlined in this manner, it's so simple it seems obvious: do community volunteer work with your friends.

Covey further explains that what we feel as role conflict, or difficulty dividing time between roles, is often shown to be perceived role conflict when the roles are defined consistently with one's values.

Looking through each of the roles defined in the previous chapter and asking "is fulfilling this role consistent with my mostly deep held values" can often yield clues about where perceived conflicts rather than actual conflicts exist. Covey also cautions against defining roles passively based on societal norms or social expectations.

Covey begins **The Power Of Goals** with some startling news to anyone interested enough in personal growth to read a time management book: there are dangers in setting goals. Covey describes two dangers of goal-setting: the damage to our integrity when we aren't able to achieve our goals and the devastation to non goal related areas of our lives that sometimes happens when we do achieve our goals.

The author describes the devastation to non goal related areas of our lives in order to reach a goal as "ladder against the wrong wall syndrome" That is, you reach your goal (climb the ladder), get to the top and realize it was placed against the wrong wall, that is, you chose the wrong goal or made the wrong goal the priority.

An obvious example of this is in the question of personal happiness. If our old friend Sam's goal is "be happy"and he hasn't actually done values clarification around this, he might assume that making more money will cause him to be more happy. His specific measurable goal might be achieving a certain position at work which enables him to make more money. However, when he achieves the goal, he might find that more money hasn't, by itself, actually increased his daily happiness or contentment with his life. He leaned his ladder against the wrong wall.

One way to create value driven goals and avoid leaning your ladder against the wrong wall is to add context to goal planning. The process for this is not very complicated. The structure for creating well-designed goals includes answering questions like:

-What are you going to accomplish?

-How are you going to accomplish it, that is, using what methods?

-How will you know if you have accomplished it? What measure will you use?

-By when will you make this happen?

To add context and ensure you've created a value driven goal include the question "why do I want to meet this goal? " or "why am I making this plan and effort?" The answer should in some way fit in with your most important roles.

Covey also introduces the idea of a **perhaps list.** Keeping a perhaps list is a way to capture ideas and thoughts about future goals and actions you might take in the future without committing yourself to that goal until you're ready.

Image via Flickr

For example, let's say Sue runs across a book at the library about planning a swim across the English Channel. Sue is an excellent swimmer and has been looking for a new physical challenge. However, she's got one semester left in graduate school so this is not the time for her to begin training for a Channel swim. However, if she adds "swim the English Channel" to her perhaps list, she won't lose the idea, nor will she set herself up for failure by starting an ill-timed goal.

Covey reminds the reader that the concept of synergy should be considered in all goal setting. Before setting any specific goal, it's important to consider if there might be another goal which could fulfill more of your roles. In the example of Sue and the Channel swim, she might consider her role as mother as well as her physical need to exercise in order to stay healthy. If she has an adult son who lives in San Francisco, she might choose instead to train for the Cross Bay Swim that takes place in the waters of San Francisco in order to spend time with her son.

Finally, Covey recommends setting weekly goals based on longer-term, context based goals. This weekly goal setting is structured through the lens of roles by asking the question "What are the one or two most important things I could do in this role this week that would have the greatest positive impact?"

In **The Perspective Of The Week** Covey continues with the discussion of weekly goals but offers more specific guidelines for using weekly planning. Weekly planning is preferable to daily planning, the authors explains, because it allows a more full perspective and decreases triggers for urgency addiction. The author uses the metaphor of trying to take a walk looking only through a telephoto lens of a camera: there is plenty of information about the smallest cracks in the sidewalk, but you can't see the overall sidewalk enough to keep yourself off the street.

Covey asserts that an important part of weekly planning is the concept of **balanced renewal** particularly weekly renewal. Covey's suggested practice of weekly renewal is earmarking out a day each week for Quadrant II activities. These specific renewal activities actually then, provide physical, emotional and spiritual refreshment. This can prevent actions taken as a part of urgency addiction. Done properly, weekly renewal also keep us from passively engaging in Quadrant IV activities (such as, again, watching endlessly reality tv) that don't actually provide much real renewal (or even joy) for most people.

Covey suggests the following as part of the Quadrant II weekly renewal activities:

-Nurturing relationships in the family and beyond

-Engaging in rest and more active recreation

-Rebuilding commitment to values by engaging in religious activities

-Building commitment to community through volunteering.

Covey also suggests an additional tool for weekly planning: the use of time blocks. Time blocks are specific periods of time set aside, usually for Quadrant II activities that aren't necessarily specifically weekly goal based. For example, if Sue wants to spend more time with her teenage daughter but doesn't have a specific activity planned, she might create a time block and map out Saturday morning as mom/daughter time, with an activity or structure to be decided later.

In **Integrity In The Moment Of Choice,** Covey explains why value driven decisions are important and presents a few techniques to enhance our effectiveness at making value driven decisions under time pressure. Our lives do not go according to plan each and every day; we are constantly called on to make decisions about how to use our time and attention. With a value-driven framework we base our decisions not on our own needs (although they may be part of the decision) or on a falsely inflated sense of urgency, but on our deeply held values and principles.

One tool Covey suggests using in order to increase our effectiveness in making decisions is to spend daily time in reflection connecting with our goals, highest values and principles. In this way, we can develop something like a sense memory of "this is what it feels like to live by the highest good."

Covey also suggests three guidelines for any decision:

-Ask with intent, that is, consider carefully what the right choice is, with the intent of doing the right thing.

-Listen without excuse. In other words, if you're going to ask yourself what the right thing to do is, actually commit to doing it, without making excuses why you can't do it.

-Act with courage. Take the action that you've determined is the right thing to do, even if you don't really feel like you want to do it.

In **Learning From Living**, Covey focuses on reviewing each week at the week's end so that you can more effectively plan the next week. The point of the weekly review is to close the learning loop, which consists of three parts: organizing, acting, and then evaluating.

Evaluating closes the loop so that what you've learned from the previous week is used to organize the next week's activities. Covey suggests using a journal to write out the answers to a lengthy list of weekly evaluation questions, including:

-Questions about goals. For example: What goals did I achieve or not achieve? What kept me from achieving those goals? Did achieving any of my goals damage my personal integrity?

-Questions about time use. For example: Did I take time for renewal? Did I take time for reflection?

-Questions about roles. For example: In what ways I able to achieve synergy between roles? How was I able live my highest values in each of my roles?

Covey also suggests that each week should be evaluated not just on the micro level by the questions above, but also through a macro lens. A macro level review includes thinking about patterns of success and failure, reappearing roadblocks to achieving goals and evaluations of patterns and processes.

The Synergy of Interdependence

Interdependence is not transactional, it's transformational. It literally changes those who are party to it. It takes into full consideration the full reality of the uniqueness and capacity of each individual.

In **The Interdependent Reality** Covey presents an alternative paradigm for human interaction based on interdependence rather than independence and applies it to achievement within the value driven time management model.

The **Independent paradigm** sees success in terms of individual achievement. However, using a interdependent paradigm all our activities are regarded as collaborative. While this might seem a mere semantic difference, what makes this paradigm so different is that requires a completely new attitude towards people with whom we share the planet.

In traditional, independent based time management systems, people are usually discussed as part of our time management problem: either we need them as resources so we can delegate or we need tools to eliminate their interruptions. The problem with time management using the independent paradigm, Covey explains, is that it simply doesn't lead to contented achievement because it doesn't work with reality. Most of what we call happiness as humans comes from our interactions with others.

Achievement at the cost of real human interaction leaves us feeling empty and completely subverts a value driven time management process. The interdependent paradigm; however, emphasizes the collaborative nature of all human activity and achievements which in turn leads to real human happiness and contentment.

First Things First enumerates three basic implications that are natural results of the interdependence paradigm. The first is that all private behavior is eventually public behavior.

To illustrate, it might be useful to revisit the earlier example of Sue, who is contemplating training for a swim across the English Channel. If Sue was using the independence paradigm to structure both her thoughts around and her planning for, the swim, she would mostly think in terms of "I." She would be solely focused on the individual nature of her achievement, and she would be inclined to measure the success or failure of her swim attempt solely on whether she made it to France.

Since the success of a Channel swim depends on many things, most importantly weather and tides over which the swimmer has no control, only a small percentage of swimmers are able to successfully finish. If Sue only measures her success in the swim by an individual achievement, that is, making it to France, there is a good chance she will be disappointed no matter how hard she trains.

If Sue uses the interdependent paradigm to plan her swim instead, her thinking will be entirely different. She will find ways to incorporate training for the Channel swim into other roles, and she will consider the relationships that she builds as a result of the training, and what she learns about people and culture from attempting the swim, all to be part of the positive outcome of her goal. This will be true regardless of whether she swims all the way to France or is has to be pulled from the water after being stung by an entire school of jellyfish within minutes of leaving England.

When she climbs into the boat, having completed her swim or having not completed her swim, her private actions (how she has treated the people along the way and how she decided to measure success and failure) will instantly become public actions. In the moments of post-swim stress and fatigue, there will be outward signs of contentment or devastation that will be obvious to everyone around.

The second implication of the interdependence paradigm is that life is one indivisible whole. Another way of saying this is that if you're lying anywhere, you're lying everywhere. Our roles overlap even when the overlap is not obvious.

The third implication of interdependence paradigm is that trust grows out of trustworthy behavior. People trust you when you consistently do what you say you will do, and when you are forthright in all your dealings.

Covey further explains that using the interdependence paradigm helps us think in terms of Quadrant II planning, because it suggests that people should always be our priority, not things. Understanding interdependence helps us redefine importance in a value driven way.

In **First Things First Together**, Covey explains how the tools, philosophies and techniques of value driven time management can be used to enhance group work. When *First Things First* principles are used in group situations, a win-win philosophy will develop that will allow collaboration, rather than competition, to rule each situation. In this way, when we use the verb "to win" it means not that someone has lost, but that group as a whole has achieved their objective.

Covey describes a three step principle driven process to achieve a win-win outcome. The first step is to think win-win. Again, this may seem like a verbal sleight of hand, but this is actually about making a fundamental change in thinking. If every encounter with every human being is based not on competition for limited resources but instead a mutually shared goal, life gets much more pleasant. As an older New Yorker once said "this city is much nicer if you thinking of it as ongoing performance art instead of 8,999,999 people competing for your subway seat"

The second step in achieving win-win situations is to seek first to understand, rather than to be understood. In this context, Covey explains, understanding is about trying to decide what is right instead of who is right.

The third step in achieving win-win is to synergize. In this context, synergizing simply means to look for third alternative solutions and develop ways to implement them using the available resources.

Covey goes on to explain that the importance of developing synergistic goals and roles in organizations is the same as for developing synergistic goals and roles in one's individual life. Individuals who are not able to synergize roles and goals within their own personal life will constantly feel torn and at war within themselves for time and attention. They will literally feel competition within themselves. Individuals who are able to develop synergistic roles and goals within their own personal life create a win-win situation wherein parts of their life serve as a catalyst for greater success.

Teams that are unable to develop synergistic roles and goals will spend most of their time in Quadrant III activities, spinning their wheels, with each member of the team unable to see where they fit as a whole and in constant competition with other team members. Teams that develop synergistic roles and goals will be able to collaborate and create more significant contributions more than any one team member could.

In order to create win-win outcomes within teams, Covey suggests creating **stewardship agreements**, or structures for decision making and work which function within a value driven framework. Stewardship agreements create synergistic partnerships to accomplish first things together. In order to create these stewardship agreements, teams must:

-Specify desired results

-Set guidelines, both for general policies and procedures around how the group works and other guidelines like known failure paths and desired levels of initiative.

-Identify the available resources and discuss how to access them

-Define accountability

-Determine the consequences, both for achieving the desired results and for not achieving the desired results.

In **Empowerment From The Inside Out**, Covey explore what type of organizations are able to transition to value driven time management and how individuals within any organization can help influence their organization to become more principle-centered. Covey calls this process empowerment from the inside out and characterizes all people in organization as having a circle of influence even if they don't have an actual leadership position.

In order for individuals to empower themselves and their circle of influence to work in Quadrant II, group members must first cultivate the conditions of empowerment.The conditions of empowerment include:

-Trustworthiness. In order to be considered trustworthy, individuals in the system must be both competent and have good character. Character includes maturity and integrity.

-Trust. Trustworthiness is the cause and trust is the effect.

-Win-win stewardship agreements. Even in high trust environments, if the structure to create positive, shared collaboration isn't present, it will be difficult for people to work together without unnecessary competition.

-Self directed individuals and teams. Leadership must consist not of supervising methods people use to achieve goals, but by holding them accountable and providing resources they need to achieve the shared goals.

-Aligned structures and systems. It's difficult to concentrate on Quadrant II activity if the structure of the entire work day is focused on Quadrant III activities. Work environments where there are frequent emergency meetings for non emergencies are an example of this.

-Accountability. Individuals and teams need to know what is expected of them and know when they have not met this expectation.

In addition to creating these favorable conditions, individuals and teams seeking to focus on Quadrant II activities must also incorporate regular feedback into the planning cycle. Finally, formal leaders in organizations transitioning to value driven time management, must see their role as leader/servant. This implies less time spent micromanaging and more time spent creating shared vision.

The Power And Peace of Principle Centered Living

In **From Time Management to Personal Leadership** and **The Peace of the Results**, Covey concludes the book with real world examples and promises of how applying the principles can help individuals find more power, peace and contentment. The principles, Covey explains, are both a valuable means to an end and an end unto themselves because they provide a structure that is consistent with deeply held values.

The power that Covey illustrates is in the day to day demands of life that require frequent changes of plan and instant decision making. For example, if we revisit Sue, we might find that when she applies the value-driven principles both to her overall planning for her English Channel swim and her daily training program, she is able to achieve her goal of swimming the Channel without sacrificing the goal of spending time with her family.

The peace that comes from living the principles and putting first things first, Covey explains, is a function of living a deep inner life. Principle-centered living creates peace in all four dimensions of life; peace of conscience, peace of mind, peace in relationships and peace in one's body. Freed of the conflict of believing one thing and living another, our daily activities bring peace instead of angst.

Additionally, Covey says, a principle-centered life is peaceful because it deals with life as it is, rather than how we perceive it should be. If we expect to accomplish just what we set out to each day, we will become frustrated and discouraged. With the principle tools at our side, we find it's easier to deal with interruptions, things going wrong and other people acting in ways we don't want them to. Freed from the expectation that days should be without challenges, we only have to deal with the challenge and not our disappointment as well.

Finally, Covey suggests a simple question to use to frame daily principle-centered life, a "if you forget everything else, please remember this" type suggestion. Every day, Covey says, ask yourself "is there something I feel I could do to make a difference"and then if there is, go do it.

In the **Mission Statement Workshop**, Covey leads the reader through a discernment process to create a personal mission statement. Covey includes a number of different perspective expanding exercises to help readers clarify their central values. Highlights of some of the suggested exercises include:

-Visualizing your eightieth birthday and considering what you would want each of the important people in your life to say about you.

-Creating a calendar broken down into future decades and filling it with brainstormed ideas of what you would like your contribution in each of those decades to be.

-Identifying the gaps between where you are now and where you would like to be and what forces are working to widen (or narrow) that gap.

-Completing a timed freewrite about your values, including such categories as peace of mind, security, health,spiritual fulfillment, friends, family, intimate relationships,travel, sense of accomplishment and respect of others.

Covey further explains that empowering mission statements represent the deepest and best within you, are based on principles of contribution and purposes higher than self-promotion and deal with all most importants roles in your life. Finally, Covey says it's important that your mission statement inspires you, not that it impresses anyone else. It should communicate to you on the most basic, essential level about your highest good.

In **A Review of the Time Management Literature**, Covey presents a more detailed analysis of the different forms and models of time management. Instead of structuring the discussion in terms of generations, as he did in earlier chapters, Covey presents several different types of time management approaches and discusses the strengths and weaknesses of each.

The Get Organized Approach is based on the idea that the biggest time management problem is chaos and if we just made enough lists and starred enough items, we would have time enough for everything we want and need to do. The strength of this approach is that it can lend clarity to daily decision making processes, but it does nothing to address the underlying problems that cause this chaos.

The Warrior Approach to time management is based entirely on the independent paradigm. The Warrior Approach evolves from the belief that if we don't do something to fight against the system that is attempting to steal our time, we will be buried by other people's demands. The Warrior Approach uses techniques such as isolation, insulation (for example, screening calls), and delegation. The advantage is that this approach does actually protect some of our time from people who would make their emergencies ours. Unfortunately it's difficult to develop any type of collaborative relationships when using a Warrior Approach to time management.

The Magic Tool Approach is based on the assumption that if we could all just get the right technology in the right hands, time management would be simple. While it's true that electronic gadgets can be helpful in structuring how we see and interact with information, this approach is very limited. Gadgets and apps can only go so far in helping plan from a principle-centered perspective. Ultimately, human introspection is needed.

List of Important People

- **A Roger Merrill**, contributor to *First Things First*, is a founding member of the Covey Leadership Center. When *First Things First* was initially published he was the vice president of Franklin Covey company. He is currently an independent business coach and consultant. In addition to contributing to to *First Things First*, he is also the author of *Connections: Quadrant II Time Management*, and the co-author of *The Nature of Leadership*. Merrill also co-authored a book with his wife, Rebecca, called *Life Matters: Creating a Dynamic Balance of Work, Family, Time, and Money.* A Roger Merill is also the past president of the Sunday School Association of the Church of Jesus Christ of the Latter Day Saints (also known as the Mormon Church)

- **Rebecca R Merrill**, contributor to *First Things First* is consistently referred to as a " mother, grandmother, homemaker" in professional biographical sketches, including the one currently maintained by Simon and Schuster, publishers of *First Things First.* Merrill co-authored *Connections: Quadrant II Time Management* as well as *Life Matters: Creating a Dynamic Balance of Work, Family, Time, and Money.* According to Simon and Schuster, she also assisted Stephen R. Covey on *The 7 Habits Highly Effective People*.

Key Terms & Definitions

Clock versus compass: Metaphorical terms used to contrast linear time management and values driven time management. The clock represents what we do and how we manage our time. The compass, in contrast, represents basic values and personally held principles.

Independent paradigm: Model of life management that defines success in terms of individual achievement.

Interdependent paradigm: Model of life management that defines success in terms of community collaboration.

Quadrant I Activities: Activities that are important and urgent, that is driven by both the clock and the compass. Examples of Quadrant I activities include deadline-driven projects, real crises, and pressing problems.

Quadrant II Activities: Activities that are important but not urgent, that is, driven by the compass and not the clock. Examples of Quadrant II activities include long range planning, preparation and activities that build relationships and community.

Quadrant III Activities: Activities that are not important but are urgent that is, driven completely by clock and not at all by the compass. Examples of Quadrant II activities include interruptions and dealing with other people's emergencies.

Quadrant IV Activities: Activities that are not important and not urgent, that is, driven by neither the compass nor the clock. Examples of these type of activities include, busywork, unneeded paperwork and escape activities such as watching reality television.

Rule of the farm: You can't grow what you don't plant, and if you wait too long to plant it, it won't grow anyway. In other words, there are real life consequences for putting things off until the last minute.

Stewardship agreements: structures for decision making and work which function within a value driven framework.

Synergy: Cooperative interaction of roles or goals in order to produce a combined effect greater than the combination would suggest.

True north principles: ultimate principles of non-relative right or wrong.

Urgency Addiction: Collective societal obsession with activities that are seen as urgent, to the exclusion of more important activities.

Interesting Facts

- Stephen Covey tweets as @StephenRCovey, mostly about business topics and principled leadership. However,, he will occasionally lapse into near poetry, for example, "A feeling of spring fills the soul…I can imagine the flowers blooming and grass sprouting. Won't be long."

- Far-right fundamentalist Christian Bud Press has taken Covey's books to task for not being Christian enough, saying that "Stephen R. Covey [is a] Mormon author whose books promote Mormonism and the New Age."

- Covey was honored by the Mormon church for ethical leadership

- The official facebook page for Stephen R Covey has nearly 80,000 likes, despite being infrequently updated and the target of much business jargon spam.

- The Franklin-Covey site provides a flash driven mission statement generator. If you're willing to give up some personal information (name, email) you can follow the prompts to find your mission in life.

- Steve Covey has ten honorary doctorates.

- In a 2004 CNN Money article, a description of Covey is included that –for no easily discernible reason– includes the phrase "Covey's bald head is shaped like an artillery shell."

- Covey's wife Sandra was the youngest member of the Mormon Tabernacle Choir on its first European tour.

- Playhouses for children are built under each stairwell of the Covey home; one has a Noah's Ark theme.

- When asked about the grandeur of his home, Covey replied: "I don't need to justify it. The Lord knows my heart,"

Sources

- A Roger Merill's Homepage: Bio

- News of the Church: Changes in Auxiliary Presidencies

- USA Today, Covey takes a lesson from himself, releases '8th Habit'

- Stephencovey.com, Personal Bio

- FranklinCovey.com, Mission Statement Builder

- Church News, Stephen R. Covey honored for ethical leadership

- Twitter, @StephenRCovey

- Simon and Schuster: Biography of Author Rebecca R Merrill

- Deception In the Church, Master List Of Cult, New Age, Pro-Homosexual And Other Non-Christian Books Being Sold In Christian Bookstores

- CNN Money, WHAT'S SO EFFECTIVE about STEPHEN COVEY? The author of The Seven Habits of Highly Effective People sells a message of moral renewal, and corporate America is buying it. Is this a good thing?

- Daily Herald, Stephen Covey to join USU's Jon M. Huntsman School of Business

- Facebook, Stephen Covey Public Figure Page

Additional Reading

- Zen Habits, Exclusive Interview: Stephen Covey on His Morning Routine, Blogs, Technology, GTD and The Secret

- The Franklin Planner Store, Products That Promote Principle Driven Time Management

- Global Dharma, Interview with Stephen Covey

- Adler Group, Behavioral vs. Performance-based Interviewing Using Stephen Covey's Seven Habits

- The Third Alternative, A Third Alternative to the Debt Crisis

Table of Contents

I. Quicklet on Stephen R. Covey's The 8th Habit: From Effectiveness to Greatness

Quicklet on Stephen R. Covey's The 8th Habit: From Effectiveness to Greatness

About the Book

Published in 2004, Stephen R. Covey's *The 8th Habit: From Effectiveness to Greatness* builds upon the his widely read *The 7 Habits of Highly Effective People* that was published 15 years earlier. The author expands his philosophy for being effective and successful in professional and personal endeavors to crossing the threshold into the realm of genius and steadfast piece of mind. *The 8th Habit* was designed to be a guide for today's "knowledge-worker society," which has a distinct set of dilemmas and social nuances with which industrial societies of years past did not have to contend.

The book's front flap boils down the core concept "The crucial challenge of our world today is this: *to find our voice and inspire others to find theirs.* It is what Covey calls the 8th Habit." This lofty philosophical world view applies to individuals, organizations, and the broader scope of modern humanity. As a *New York Times* book reviewer noted about Covey, "His premise is that most of us are battling to feel engaged and fulfilled. To achieve what we seek, we must find our 'voice,' a concept that has four components." The all-important voice that serves as Covey's conceptual cornerstone is made up of talent, passion, need, and conscience.

This book is more philosophically abstract and delves much deeper into the individual as well as collective psyche of this modern knowledge-driven world of ours. It was written to address the current reality that most people aren't thriving and realizing their full potential and as a result feel listless and unfulfilled. A DVD accompanies the print version of the *8th Habit* in an attempt to help readers and viewers discover their uniqueness and personal significance amid the current challenging and rapidly shifting socio-economic reality.

Though the book is predominantly consumed by members of the corporate business community and those who work in large government organizations. One CEO had this to say about *The 8th Habit:*

"Stephen Covey is able to bring out the importance of building habits that can take an organisation to greatness in a global world of business...[They] helped me focus and also reinforced many beliefs that help move us along the path to building a great organisation.

[The book] is a tonic for today's corporate leaders and helps empower teams and build leaders." (*Financial Times*, In full: Experts choose their favorite reads)

About the Author

Stephen R. Covey is the co-founder and vice chairman of FranklinCovey Co., a firm that does training and management consulting for businesses and other types of organizations around the world.

"Recognized as one of *Time* magazine's 25 most influential Americans, Stephen R. Covey has dedicated his life to demonstrating how every person can truly control their destiny with profound, yet straightforward guidance. As an internationally respected leadership authority, family expert, teacher, organizational consultant, and author, his advice has given insight to millions." (*StephenCovey.com*, About Dr. Covey)

According to his website, Covey's books have sold more than 20 million copies in 38 languages. His other titles include: *The 7 Habits of Highly Effective People, The 7 Habits of Highly Effective Families, The Nature of Leadership, First Things First, Principle-Centered Leadership,* and *The 3rd Alternative.* He holds an MBA from Harvard University, a doctorate degree from Brigham Young University, as well as eight honorary doctorates and awards such as the International Entrepreneur of the Year Award, International Man of Peace Award, and the National Fatherhood Award. He is on the board of the Points of Light Foundation and is a frequent lecturer on the concepts presented in his books.

A father of nine with 44 grandchildren, Covey and his wife live in the Rocky Mountains of Utah (Covey, *The 8th Habit*). Steve Forbes, a corporate executive and business magazine editor, described Covey as "...a sure-footed guide to those desiring to better themselves" (*The 8th Habit*).

Overall Summary

Covey delivers more than 400 pages, 15 chapters, and eight appendices on viable techniques that can help leaders maximize their organizations' productivity and potential for success. The author, who is known for intricately structured and well-organized book formats, also subdivides *The 8th Habit* into a three-chapter introductory section, Part 1 called "Find Your Voice," and Part 2 titled "Inspire Others to Find Their Voice," which is further subdivided into sections such as "Focus—Modeling and Pathfinding," "Execution—Aligning and Empowering," and "The Age of Wisdom." There is also a 10-page question-and-answer section that addresses issues such as the practical application of the book's habit-changing and habit-forming conceptual techniques and questions related to the moral elements on which Covey writes.

A very central theme in *The 8th Habit* is the importance of sharing the knowledge on attaining effectiveness and greatness with others. By no means is this a guidebook for isolated self-interest and individual personal gain. Covey applies his philosophies to the big picture far beyond the individual via Part 2, which is the bulk of the book's content. He places great emphasis on how to optimally function and thrive within the culture of a particular organization or an even broader social culture. From a leadership perspective, Covey outlines ways to proactively, rather than competitively, enact procedures aimed at attaining goals.

A *USA Today* profile on Covey describes *The 8th Habit* as a sequel to his 1989 best-seller *The 7 Habits of Highly Effective People* (No. 22 of the 25 most influential business books according to *Time* magazine). Covey's seven effective habits call for being proactive; starting with an end-game in mind; putting "first things first"; approach endeavors with a "win-win" mentality; seeking first to understand, then to be understood"; create synergy; and practice and prioritize acts of personal renewal (FranklinCoveySouthAsia.com, 7 Habits Wite Paper). "While those habits are still relevant, Covey says the emergence of a new Information/Knowledge Worker Age—fueled by the Internet, automation and outsourcing of manufacturing jobs—requires the addition of an eighth habit..." (*Newsweek*, Quick Read).

As noted earlier according to Covey, "The 8th Habit, then, is not about adding one more habit to the 7—one that somehow got forgotten. It's about seeing and harnessing the power of *a third dimension* to the 7 Habits that meets *the* central challenge of the Knowledge Worker Age. This 8th Habit is to *Find Your Voice and Inspire Others to Find Theirs"* (*The 8th Habit*). Covey goes on to define voice as "*unique personal significance*... that is revealed as we face our greatest challenges and which makes us equal to them."

The 8th Habit comes with a DVD that contains short films referenced in each chapter. These videos serve as examples that illustrate Covey's concepts and are designed to work in tandem with the print content. The author sets up the videos' basic ideas but also urges readers to watch them in their entirety to most thoroughly grasp the information he seeks to convey.

Chapter by Chapter Summary and Analysis

Chapter 1: The Pain

"The Pain" analyzed in this chapter refers to the frustration, confusion, lack of direction, and confidence, pressure, and emptiness that many professional people feel in today's fast-paced, technology-driven workplace. Toward remedying these emotional and psychological ills, Covey provides his first explanation of the antidote that forms the crux of *The 8th Habit*: finding one's voice. The chapter includes a diagram and written explanation that describes the "voice" as "unique personal significance." It is at the central connecting point of a person's passions and talents fulfilling a particular need presented by the world at large backed by the individual's conscience, which Covey describes as "that still, small voice within that assures you of what is right and that prompts you to actually do it."

The story of Muhammad Yunus, founder of a bank that extends microcredit loans to the poor of Bangladesh, is an example of "the voice" in action as the way to transcend from the negativity described early in the chapter. Yunus saw the potential of establishing a microloan system to predominantly female artisans who lived in the nation's many small villages and started as a loan guarantor, providing them with small bits of capital to start a small business, such as one woman's bamboo-stool enterprise. Covey writes: "At the heart of this empowerment lies individual women who chose individually and in synergistic norm-producing groups to become self-reliant, independent entrepreneurs producing goods out of their own homes or neighborhoods or backyards to become economically viable and successful. They *found* their voices."

Chapter 2: The Problem

The age of the knowledge worker is upon us, and it is this transition stage between this new professional and economic paradigm and the previous industrial age from where the world is now emerging that is the cause of the pains discussed in Chapter 1. The mentality of the industrial age that valued *things* such as manufacturing machines as an investment and the workers who operated them as an expense to the company has a negative effect on the new age where human knowledge and talent is a company's most valuable asset. Rather than valuing a worker's able body as was the case in the industrial age, now the whole person—"body, mind, heart and spirit"—must be satisfied in order to achieve the utmost productivity and personal well-being.

Covey uses the short film *Max & Max* as an example of how micromanaging workers and the control philosophy of management that has its roots in the industrial age "thing" mindset. This is a sure way to create a codependent culture within an organization that drains its people of initiative and leadership qualities. This suppression of human talent and voice results in low productivity and the personal pains described in Chapter 1. Because human nature is largely driven by a person's ability to make choices with regard to their thinking and actions, it is crucial for managers and leaders to create a setting that fulfills each human element—again, a worker or group member's body, mind, heart and spirit.

Chapter 3: The Solution

The first three chapters of *The 8th Habit* are brief and very on point. Covey avoids superfluous language and instead offers very direct, cut-to-the-chase prose that seems quite logically tailored to an audience of readers who don't have all that much reading time. These introductory chapters also set the tone for the rest of the book's content, which incorporates lots of graphics to illustrate and highlight concepts.

Chapter 3 focuses on setting up the ideas that are more thoroughly examined in subsequent chapters. In short, "the solution" to the pains and problems of modern society and business is discovering and expressing one's voice by gaining a solid understanding of personal identity, then showing others how to get in touch with their own unique talents and gifts.

A British writer suffering from writer's block is this chapter's example of someone who found his voice as he overcame his creative shutdown and went on to invent a successful and socially relevant story. Amid his despair and mounting debts, the writer took to walking the streets of London at night, where he witnessed intensely abject poverty and the corresponding social ills.

"Gradually, the full reality of what he was seeing began to hit him—the impact of selfishness and greed and those who would take advantage of others. An idea touched his heart and began to grow in his mind…He returned to his writing with an energy and enthusiasm he had never known…His whole life had changed. He'd truly found his voice."

Part 1: Find Your Voice

Chapter 4: Discover Your Voice—Unopened Birth-Gifts

Covey defines "birth-gifts" as an individual's talents, capacities, privileges, intelligences, and opportunities that for the most part remain untapped without a specific, chosen effort to unleash them. The three most important birth-gifts are the ability to make choices, the unchanging natural laws or principles that guide nature, and humanity's four intelligences that relate to four components of human nature—physical/economic, emotional/social, mental, and spiritual. By gaining awareness of these fundamental aspects of life, especially the greatly empowering effect that grasping the freedom of choice elicits, an individual is primed to discover their voice and go on to achieve great success and happiness.

This chapter features several anecdotal cases-in-point on the three birth-gifts. The example of choice takes the form of an employee choosing not to run away from dealing with a difficult boss, but instead focusing attention on establishing a trust-based, productive relationship with him. Covey challenges readers "to reflect on that space that exists between stimulus and response, and to use it wisely in enlarging your freedoms and keeping yourself constantly growing, learning and contributing." A film on the book's DVD titled *The Law of the Harvest* shows the metaphorical connection between nature's harvest cycle and the "human character, human greatness and all human relationships." Another video about an elementary school that incorporated Covey's philosophy into its curriculum reflects the importance of nurturing the four intelligences. "The whole concept behind Finding Your Voice and Inspiring Others to Find Theirs is a synergistic concept," Covey wrote. "It is the integration of our intelligences and capacities, which unleashes human potential."

Chapter 5: Express Your Voice—Vision, Discipline, Passion and Conscience

Here Covey more deeply analyzes the four inherent human intelligences discussed in the previous chapter. "The highest manifestations of these four intelligences are: for the mental, *vision;* for the physical, *discipline;* for the emotional, *passion;* for the spiritual, *conscience.* These manifestations also represent our highest means of *expressing our voice.*" Vision, discipline, and passion are the time-immemorial mark of a leader who has had great effect on current as well as future generations of followers. When conscience (or "moral authority") enters the equation as a guiding force for the other intelligences, then changing the world in a positive way ensues. A summary of Part I closes chapter 5 by succinctly capsulating the ideas presented thus far. Covey wrote:

"I commend to you again this simple way of thinking about life: a whole person (body, mind, heart and spirit) with four basic needs (to live, to learn, to love, to leave a legacy), and four intelligences or capacities (physical, mental, emotional and spiritual) and their highest manifestations (discipline, vision, passion, conscience), all of which represent the four dimensions of voice (need, talent, passion and conscience). As we respect, develop, integrate and balance these intelligences and their highest manifestations, the synergy between them lights *the fire within* us and we find our voice."

The story of a man from Uganda in the accompanying video called *Stone* embodies the power of the conscience to direct one's vision, discipline and passion. Despite a devastating knee injury that abruptly cancelled the young man's promising future career as a professional soccer player, he chose to dedicate himself to providing aid and comfort to disadvantaged Ugandan youths. By connecting with his birth-gifts, Stone overcame the temptations of revenge and self-pity and instead committed himself wholeheartedly to making the necessary sacrifices and exerting the personal discipline needed to realize his goal of passing on his uplifting, personally fulfilling world view to the young men to whom he reached out, teaching them to govern their lives via the "principles (conscience) of self-mastery, training and contribution" (Covey, *The 8th Habit*).

Part 2: Inspire Others to Find Their Voice

Chapter 6: Inspiring Others to Find Their Voice—The Leadership Challenge

Part 2 begins with a succinctly stated definition of leadership: "communicating to people their worth and potential so clearly that they come to see it in themselves." Within the context of an organization, Covey also supplies readers with a second easily referenced definition: "an organization is made up of individuals who have a *relationship* and a *shared purpose.*" The term "management" pertains to "things without the freedom to choose," such as money, facilities, equipment, time, and information. "Leadership," however, applies directly to people who are of course governed by human nature with whom a person in a position of authority has a direct relationship. The key function of leadership is dealing with change and identifying, then mitigating, both "acute" and "chronic" problems. Four distinct roles of leadership entail: "modeling" (setting a good example guided by conscience); "pathfinding" (determining the organization's course with the creative input of colleagues by applying vision); "aligning" (establishing and maintaining systems to remain on course using discipline); and "empowering" (with passion as a guiding force, "focus talent on results, not methods, then get out of people's way and give help as requested").

To expound on the importance of organized, sequential action as the proper means of expressing effective leadership, the author offers what he calls "a sports metaphor," which basically states that before an athlete can hone his or her actual playing skills for a particular sport, muscle strength and endurance must be present. "When a player goes to a professional training camp out of shape…he is simply unable to develop the intended *skills.* And if he can't develop the skills, there is no way he can become a useful member of a *team* and part of a winning system." In an organizational context, personal development must come before creating trusting relationships. Trusting relationships must exist before an organization can become "characterized by teamwork, cooperation and contribution to the wider community."

Focus—Modeling and Pathfinding

Chapter 7: The Voice of Influence—Be a Trim-Tab

Modeling is the core element for all leadership endeavors and is at work before and at all times during the other three leadership roles outlined in Chapter 6. It doesn't just apply to one person in a leadership position, but rather to the entire organizational team. "When you have a team of people that builds on each individual's strengths and organizes to make individual weaknesses irrelevant, you have true power in an organization," Covey wrote. Leadership is not a quality strictly reserved for those in the role of "boss." Workers at all levels should exhibit leadership if an organization is going to thrive. Covey's "7 Levels of Initiative or Self-Empowerment" provide a guiding continuum:

- Wait until told
- Ask
- Make a recommendation
- "I intend to"
- Do it and report immedeately
- Do it and report periodically
- Do it

The metaphoric concept of being a **trim-tab**, which literally is a smaller rudder within the larger rudder that actually moves a boat in one direction or another, illustrates how modeling affects a leader's efficacy. A video on the book's DVD profiles the nation of Mauritius, which shows that not only individuals or organizations can act as trim-tabs, but an entire nation or society can as well. Although Mauritius has had some ups and downs in its quest to break the cycle of political violence and social strife, "the real point of the story…is not that Mauritius is a perfect society; it is that *whatever* challenges we may face...we can work within our Circle of Influence and creatively 'trim-tab' our way through them" (Covey, *The 8th Habit*).

Chapter 8: The Voice of Trustworthiness—Modeling Character and Competence

Personal and professional integrity, a leader's character, is an extremely important factor affecting an organization's performance. "Trust is the glue of organizations," according to Covey, who identifies three sources from which it derives: "the personal, the institutional, and one person consciously choosing to *give* it to another—an act that leads me to *feel* your belief that I can add value." Living in praxis Covey's *7 Habits of Highly Effective People* (See "Overall Summary" above) is the essence of developing personal character. This is the means by which leaders establish character credibility with their workforce or team members. A "Personal Planning System" tool that involves consitently writing down the things that are most important to you during varying long-term and short-term time frames is the key to developing focus that leads to execution of your highest priorities.

The "Big Rocks" film on the book's DVD show a metaphoric example of balancing priorities into a comprehensible scheme that is easy to follow. The exercise comes from Covey's seminars. The size of a stone equates to the importance of a particular priority in one's life.

"*Put the big rocks first.* If you fill your bowl or your life with pebbles first, and then you have a major crisis with one of your children, a financial or health setback, or a significant new creative opportunity, what are you going to do? Those things are big rocks, and there is no room left for them in your life. Always think in terms of big rocks first." (Covey, *The 8th Habit*)

Basing decisions around the "big rocks" is a sure-fire way to eliminate angst when circumstances require you to say "no" to things that seem pressing but not as crucial as your main priorities.

Chapter 9: The Voice and Speed of Trust

Trust is the most important component of any relationship. It expedites communication by removing the hampering effect of doubt. "It is the glue that holds organizations, cultures and relationships together...It is the fruit of regular actions inspired by the conscience and the heart," Covey states, and it must be accompanied by the values of humility and respect. Establishing lasting trust follows this dynamic, labeled "deposits" in the "emotional bank account":

- Seek first to understand another person's perspective

- Honesty and integrity must frame all interaction.
- Kindness and courtesies—the "little things" in life matter profoundly.
- Think "win-win or no deal."
- Clarify expectations.
- Be loyal to those who aren't present—never speak ill of someone behind their back.
- Apologize—never let the ego prevent you from saying you're sorry or admitting faults.
- Give and receive feedback—never shy away from giving negative feedback in a constructive way, and don't be put off when you receive it in the same manner.
- "Forgiveness involves forgetting, letting it go, and moving on."

The film "Teacher" on the DVD is about Helen Keller, who was deaf and blind, and her teacher, Anne Sullivan, who was blind and also had a rough childhood in her own right. Covey advises:

"As you watch this film…study it through the lens of the two roads—the upper road to greatness and the lower road to mediocrity…Study how the relationship of trust between Anne and Helen was formed through constant deposits, study the speedy, subtle communication that was enabled—the patience, the persistence, the understanding—and the bonding that took place…It is a beautiful story of two magnificent persons who found their own voices and devoted their lives to inspiring others to find theirs…"

Chapter 10: Blending Voices—Searching for the Third Alternative

Conflict resolution is a creative skill based "upon the *moral authority* at the personal level and *trust* in relationships," according to Covey. Approaching adversarial situations with a win-win mindset and a genuine commitment to understanding the perspective of others, then employing bona fide listening skills toward gaining a viable understanding of the circumstances is the key to realizing what Covey calls the "Third Alternative." The driving force for attaining the Third Alternative is communication with a particular emphasis on its listening aspect. Two nonsequential steps must be taken in order to reach the synergy needed for the Third Alternative to come to fruition:

- "Would you be willing to search for a solution that is better than what either one of you (us) have proposed?"
- "Would you agree to a simple ground rule: No one can make his or her point until they have restated the other person's point to his or her satisfaction."

An example of synergistic, third-alternative solutions is evidenced in the video "Street Hawkers" on the book's DVD. It tells the story of a South African company that opened a clothing retail store in an old section of a city that was traditionally occupied by street vendors who sold fruits and vegetables. Instead of calling police to clear out the street hawkers who crowded in front of the store on its opening day, making a mess and blocking its front entrance, the store manager instead sought a Third Alternative. He discussed things with the vendors, then expressed his needs. "Together, this most unlikely team of retail managers and street hawkers developed a synergistic plan that worked for both of them" (Covey, *The 8th Habit*).

Chapter 11: One Voice—Pathfinding Shared Vision, Values and Strategy

Pathfinding is a means to creating organization without expressly, authoritatively demanding it. All members of a team must have input into a group's mission, otherwise full and unanimous commitment to it will invariably lag. Through focused and empowering communication, all involved will agree on the necessary criteria that will guide all subsequent decisions related to the organization's course of action. Covey lists four realities with which a leader must contend in order to properly execute pathfinding:

- **Market realities**—internal perceptions and external forces that affect an organization's function.
- **Core competencies**—determining the inherent strengths that pertain to the nexus between an organization's best abilities, its primary passions, and market demand, as well as the input of one's conscience or spirit that results in a found voice leading the way toward mission fulfillment.
- **Stakeholder Wants and Needs**—taking into consideration the interests of various factions that are relevant to a particular organization, for example from target customers, to the owners, to employees, and to the broader community and natural environment.
- **Values**—"Most people...haven't developed the criteria that will inform and govern all other decisions, and now we're trying to do it for an entire group...Think how complex that is, how interdependent—really, how challenging" (Covey, *The 8th Habit*).

The film "Goal!" on the DVD reveals a parallel between trying to get young children to play a somewhat coherent, organized game of soccer and trying to get co-workers to stay focused on the same overarching organizational goal.

Another real-life example of effective pathfinding can be found in the impressive operation of Ritz-Carlton hotels. The company's culture creator, former president and COO Horst Shulze, had this to add to Covey's discourse: "As a businessperson, I am obligated to create an environment where people feel part of something, feel fulfilled, and have purpose. It is purpose—it is value in their lives—that leads people to truly give of their minds." The crux of Shulze's sentiment is that all workers should be encouraged to contribute their knowledge in their particular area of operation toward maximizing productivity and as a result will feel like an integral, important part of the group's overall mission.

Execution—Aligning and Empowering

Chapter 12: The Voice and Discipline of Execution—Aligning Goals and Systems for Results

This chapter addresses the complex question of "how do we execute both values and strategy consistently without relying on the formal leader's continuing presence to keep everyone going in the right direction?" Alignment, which needs constant attention, is the answer, which means coming up with and instituting systems and structures that bolster an organization's core values and most important priorities. It is crucial to establish organizational trustworthiness in addition to personal trustworthiness. This is achieved by avoiding contradictory strategies such as promoting cooperation and teamwork while simultaneously sponsoring incentives based on competition among employees, according to Covey. "Feedback systems" are the tool through which an organization's state of alignment is assessed.

The book's DVD contains a film called "Berlin Wall" that examines the adjustment Germans went through as the relative economic security of Communism gave way to the freedoms but lessened job security of a capitalist system. Covey preps readers/viewers to "think of how truly difficult it is for people to develop a new mind-set, a new paradigm, a new and different way of thinking—how it requires a new skill-set and a new tool-set." The author also points out the futility of attempting to teach new things with an old mindset, stressing the importance of grasping a fresh way of thinking in addition to utilizing new technology or thriving within a new political and economic paradigm.

Chapter 13: The Empowering Voice—Releasing Passion and Talent

Focusing empowerment techniques on the power to choose is much more effective in the 21st century economy than the "carrot and stick" method that was the norm of the bygone industrial age, which Covey equates to "animal psychology." The author fuses empowerment with the previously discussed concepts:

"*Modeling* principle-centered trustworthy behavior inspires trust without 'talking it.' *Pathfinding* creates order without demanding it. *Aligning* nourishes both vision and empowerment without proclaiming them. *Empowerment* is the fruit of the other three. It is the natural result of both personal and organizational trustworthiness, which enables people to identify and unleash their human potential."

The "Win-Win Agreement Process" is Covey's empowering tool. It is a flexible, psychological and social contract that expressly defines expectations between a boss and employee. This is not a written document, but rather a creative and adaptable understanding that "is written first into the hearts and minds of people."

"The Case of the Janitors (Turning Manual Workers into Knowledge Workers)" is a poignant illustration of empowerment. It demonstrates that if, through empowerment techniques, you can have "whole" people working a whole job that is "menial, unskilled, and low-paid," it can happen in any occupation (Covey, *The 8th Habit*). As a result of a management development instructor's training of first-level supervisors to better motivate their janitorial crew, which was suffering from low productivity and discipline problems, after a relatively short time "quality went up, job turnover and discipline problems went way down, social norms developed around initiative, cooperation, diligence and quality, and job satisfaction increased significantly" (Covey, *The 8th Habit*). This was because the maintenance supervisor engaged more of the janitors' hearts and minds by consistently giving them more say in the planning, execution and evaluation of their work.

The Age of Wisdom

Chapter 14: The 8th Habit and the Sweet Spot

Early in Chapter 14, Covey states: "The reason why the 8th Habit is such an idea is that it embodies an understanding of the whole person—an understanding that gives its possessors *the* key to crack open the limitless potential of the knowledge worker economy." This all-important mindset for the working world of today very vividly equips practitioners to see the potential in others. It is leadership that so clearly conveys to people their worth and potential that they are able to see it within themselves. With regard to execution, Covey provides four "Disciplines" toward putting 8th-Habit theory into practice:

- Focus on the wildly important
- Create a compelling scoreboard
- Translate lofty goals into specific actions
- Hold each other accountable all of the time

The DVD's video titled "It's Not Just Important, It's Wildly Important!" is a collection of interviews with actual clients of Covey's consulting firm. "It illustrates the misalignment and lack of goal clarity that pervades most organizations" (Covey, *The 8th Habit*). This is a telling example that many viewers may see as all too familiar when comparing the testimonials with what goes on in their own organizations or companies. Apply this chapter's prescriptions for focus and execution problems in order to critically assess solutions to the various problems that most organizations experience.

Chapter 15: Using Our Voices Wisely to Serve Others

The "Age of Wisdom" is nearly upon us, Covey boldly states: "It will come about either through the force of circumstance that humbles people, or through the force of conscience—or perhaps both." He further defines this concept as the fusion between knowledge and information and purpose and principles. In the telling "Conclusion" section of this, the book's final chapter, Covey sums up his central intention for *The 8th Habit*:

"This book has primarily attempted to teach one basic paradigm: that people are *whole people*—body, mind, heart and spirit. As a person engages in the *sequential 8th Habit process* of finding one's own voice, making the choice to expand her influence by inspiring others to find their voice, she increases her freedom and power of choice to solve her greatest challenges and serve human needs; she learns how *leadership can eventually become a choice* not a position, so that leadership, the enabling art, is widely distributed throughout organizations and society, and therefore, while we manage or control things, we lead (empower) people."

The video "Gandhi," an excerpt from the Hollywood film on the book's DVD, displays "a person of weakness and pride, but also a person who used his birth-gifts to develop humility, courage, integrity, discipline and vision" (Covey, *The 8th Habit*). Gandhi is a historical figure who very poignantly exemplifies someone whose life is a shining example of 8th-Habit living. Never elected to any kind of formal authority, Covey points out that, as Gandhi himself observed, "any ordinary person who used his or her powers could do the same thing"—effect profound influence for the good of his people and the whole of mankind.

Important People

George Washington is a good exemplar of the 8th Habit. His vision, discipline, and passion played an extremely important role in establishing America as a new nation during the height of the age of European colonial empires.

Florence Nightingale was the founder of modern nursing practices worked tirelessly her whole adult life to improve the quality of nursing in military medical facilities. "Her vision and passion overcame her personal reticence" (Covey, *The 8th Habit*).

Mohandas K. Gandhi was a major player in India's independence from the British Empire despite that fact that he never held elected office and no formal position of popular leadership. "Gandhi's moral authority created such strong social and cultural norms that it ultimately shaped political will," Covey wrote. "He governed his life by an awareness of a universal conscience that resided within the people, the international community, and the British themselves."

Margaret Thatcher became the first female leader of a leading industrial nation. Though her critics abound, "she was passionate about urging people to assume the discipline of personal responsibility and to build self-reliance, and she was passionate about bolstering free enterprise in her country," according to Covey. "During her tenure in British politics, she helped lift Britain out of economic recession."

Nelson Mandela survived nearly three decades in prison for opposing the South African apartheid regime and went on to become president of the nation. "Mandela was impelled by his imagination rather than by his memory. He could envision a world far beyond the confines of his experience and memory...Deep within his soul resonated a belief in the worth of every South African citizen" (Covey, *The 8th Habit*).

Mother Teresa was the epitome of someone who wholly dedicated her entire being to serving the needs of the poor. "She bequeathed her highly disciplined upholding of vows of poverty, purity and obedience upon her organization, which has both grown and strengthened even since her passing" (Covey, *The 8th Habit*).

Horst Shulze is a successful business manager who was instrumental in creating the corporate culture that fueled the success of the Ritz-Carlton hotel chain. In an interview with Covey, he said "Leadership creates an environment that makes people want to, rather than have to, do. It is a business imperative to create that environment" (*The 8th Habit*).

Joshua Lawrence Chamberlain was a Civil War military hero of the battle at Gettysburg who led the Union's 20th Maine Company of volunteers. He received a slew of military and congressional honors. Upon receiving a magnificent stallion as a gift years later, he remarked "in characteristic humility and self-deprecation...'No sacrifice or service of mine requires any other reward than that which conscience gives to every man who does his duty'" (Covey, *The 8th Habit*).

Key Terms and Definitions

Trim-Tab—A smaller rudder on a boat or plane that causes a part of a larger rudder to move, which in turn actually moves the craft. In terms of a metaphoric application to individual involved in an organization, "They can move themselves and their team or department in sucha way that it positively affects the entire organization" (Covey, *The 8th Habit*).

The Third Alternative—This refers to a mutually beneficial middle ground that hinges on a win-win approach to professional and personal relations. "A third alternative is what the Buddhists call the middle way—a higher middle position that is better than either of the other two ways, like the tip of a triangle" (Covey, *The 8th Habit*).

Alignment—"*Designing and executing systems and structures that reinforce* the core values and highest strategic priorities of the organization (selected in the pathfinding process)." (Covey, *The 8th Habit*).

Moral Authority—This somewhat paradoxical term, as Covey defines it, centers on character strengths that translate into credibility in the eyes of those working under a particular leader:

"The dictionary discusses authority in terms of command, control, power, sway, rule, supremacy, domination, dominion, strength, might. But the antonym is civility, servitude weakness, follower. Moral authority is the gaining of influence through following principles. Moral dominion is achieved through servanthood, service, and contribution. Power and moral supremacy emerge from humility, where the greatest becomes the servant of all. Moral authority or primary greatness is achieved through sacrifice." (*The*

8th Habit)

Interesting Related Facts

FranklinCovey company offers consulting and training services in 123 countries. It is publicly traded on the New York Stock Exchange and caters to "90 percent of the Fortune 100, more than 75 percent of the Fortune 500, thousands of small and midsized businesses, as well as numerous government entities and educational institutions" (Covey, *The 8th Habit*).

Covey is a Mormon originally from Salt Lake City, Utah.

A Harris Poll that surveyed 23,000 U.S. residents who worked full time in key industries and key functional areas cited in *The 8th Habit* found the following:

"Only 37 percent said they have a clear understanding of what their organization is trying to achieve and why."

"Only half were satisfied with the work they have accomplished at the end of the week."

"Only 15 percent said they worked in a high-trust environment."

"Only 20 percent fully trusted the organization the work for."

"Only 13 percent have high-trust, highly cooperative working relationships with other groups."

"Only 10 percent felt that their organization holds people accountable for results."

With regard to the timely relevance of *The 8th Habit,* Covey begins Chapter 2 with this observation by Peter Drucker, who he bills as one of today's most influential managment thinkers:

"'In a few hundred years, when the history of our time is written from long-term perspective, it is likely that the most important event those historians will see is not technology, not the Internet, not e-commerce. It is an unprecedented change in the human condition. For the first time—literally—substantial and rapidly growing numbers of people have choices. For the first time, they will have to manage themselves. And society is totally unprepared for it.'"

Covey was a professor of organizational behavior and business management at Brigham Young University, and his most successful book, *The 7 Habits of Highly Effective People*, made it to no. 1 on *The New York Times* Bestseller List (Sterling International Speakers Inc., Stephen R. Covey).

Covey's latest book, published in October 2011, is *The 3rd Alternative: Solving Life's Most Difficult Problems* (*Forbes,* Stephen R. Covey Gives You a 3rd Alternative).

Sources

- Stephen R. Covey, *The 8th Habit: From Effectiveness to Greatness*
- *The New York Times*, As Successor to '7 Habits,' No. 8 Charts a New Course
- *Financial Times*, In full: Experts choose their favorite reads
- *StephenCovey.com*, About Dr. Covey
- *USA Today*, Covey takes a lesson from himself, releases '8th Habit'
- *Time*, The 25 Most Influential Business Books
- FranklinCoveySouthAsia.com, 7 Habits White Paper
- *Newsweek*, Quick Read
- Sterling International Speakers Inc., Stephen R. Covey
- *Forbes*, Stephen R. Covey Gives You a 3rd Alternative

Additional Reading

- Covey, Stephen R., First Things First: To Live, to Love, to Learn, to Leave a Legacy
- *Huffington Post*, A Third Alternative to the Debt Crisis? & A 3rd Alternative: A Super Solution for the Super Committee
- *The New York Times*, Top Author Shifts E-Book Rights to Amazon.com
- *Personal Branding Blog*, Personal Branding Interview: Stephen R. Covey

Table of Contents

I.   Stephen Covey's Great Work, Great Career

Stephen Covey's Great Work, Great Career

A Rapidly Changing World: The Historical Context of Great Work, Great Career

"The landscape of the economy is undergoing a seismic shift, and with it the landscape of opportunity. . . . You are no longer bound by the old mindset that you're just a cog in a machine."

Great Work, Great Career was published in late 2009 by FranklinCovey Publishing. This book represents one of the more recent written works by well known business mind, writer, lecturer, and motivator Stephen R. Covey, and is unique in that Covey didn't author it on his own. He enlisted the help of FranklinCovey Chief Learning Officer Jennifer Colosimo, who co-authored *Great Work, Great Career*.

Throughout the text, Covey and Colosimo attempt to teach individuals how to build careers for themselves that are both personally and financially meaningful. In doing so, this book responds to two critical cultural-historical occurrences: the United States' recent economic recession and the emergence of what the authors refer to as the "Knowledge Age."

Characterized by company downsizing and the constant threat of unemployment, the historical period in which this book is published is one of uncertainty for many professionals. Covey and Colosimo address these anxieties by arguing that companies are laying off employees because as the times change, so too do the needs of companies. If potential employees understand this shift, they can use it to their advantage by focusing on the new needs of potential employers. In the end, this ultimately presents an abundance of opportunities for those seeking to build a strong career.

The shift being referred to is the shift from the Industrial Age to the Knowledge Age. Workers of the Industrial Age were essentially tools or mechanical components, filling a job description and nothing more. But in today's Knowledge Age, employees must be creative in identifying and marketing their unique and personal sets of skills, training, and interests. Covey and Colosimo assert that by focusing on these unique characteristics, potential employees can come up with valuable and relevant solutions to a company's problems, thereby making themselves not only marketable but completely irreplaceable to the company that hires them.

The practical advice shared and the principles taught in *Great Work, Great Career* are all connected to the recent economic changes of the recession and the morphing corporate landscape of the Knowledge Age. With this cultural-historical understanding in place, readers will be better prepared to make sense of what this book has to offer.

About The Authors

"You will spend much of your life and energy on your career, so doesn't it make sense to envision and design a great career for yourself?"

Stephen R. Covey was born in 1932. After receiving an MBA from Harvard University, he began establishing himself as an innovative business mind. In particular, Covey is best known for his principles-based approach to leadership, business achievement, and time management. In 1989, he wrote his most famous book, *The 7 Habits of Highly Effective People*, which helped him "[achieve] international acclaim . . . and has sold around 12 million copies worldwide" (*White Dove Books,* Biography of Stephen R Covey). Covey is also co-founder of FranklinCovey, an international organization aimed at providing business and leadership training, along with business and time management tools and products. Since the success of *7 Habits,* Covey has written several other successful self-help books. He continues to speak at training seminars, lectures, and conferences around the world.

Via Portal Abras, *Creative Commons*

Jennifer Colosimo served as Chief Learning Officer of FranklinCovey at the time that *Great Work, Great Career* was written and published. She entered the world of business and leadership training after receiving a Bachelor's degree from University of Utah, and a Master's degree in organizational communication from Purdue University. Since then, her work at FranklinCovey and other organizations has focused on creating and teaching strategies for values-based business management and leadership.

Through speaking, lecturing, and co-authoring *Great Work, Great Career,* Colosimo has established herself as an authority when it comes to developing, teaching, and implementing innovative management techniques. According to *Premiere Speakers Bureau,* Colosimo is especially "known for making complex ideas and strategies understandable and executable; approaching opportunities with a whole person paradigm of body, mind, heart, and spirit" (Jennifer Colosimo Bio). She is also highly interested and "involved in organizations focused on the leadership development of girls, achieving self-sufficiency, and eliminating poverty" (*Jennifer Colosimo,* About Jennifer).

Life In The Knowledge Age: An Overall Summary Of Great Work, Great Career

"The landscape has never been greener. The volatile, burned-over economy of the new century provides opportunities no one ever dreamed of."

The world is changing. Once localized markets are now part of a vast and global economy. Yet this very economy is also becoming increasingly unpredictable and volatile. Technology develops and advances at increasingly rapid rates, and the Internet makes limitless stores of information available at the world's fingertips.

A result of all these important changes is that companies are now facing new challenges, problems, and needs. The old job descriptions no longer adequately address these needs, and so more and more employees are being laid off. Even while these trends may introduce fear and uncertainty to the minds of many people, *Great Work, Great Career* is clear in its assertion that opportunities for meaningful jobs and productive careers not only still exist, but are actually more plentiful than ever before.

The key to taking full advantage of these opportunities is to learn how to locate a company's specific needs and problems, and then understand how to apply your unique and personal strengths to creating a solution. When you can do this, argues Covey and Colosimo, you will always be an attractive employee to companies, regardless of hiring and economic trends.

Great Work, Great Career is essentially aimed at "[outlining] the ways in which individuals can change the way they think and act about their career and take action to transform their career from one of mediocre performance to one of great performance" (*Business Book Summaries*, Great Work, Great Career). Throughout the entire book, the authors direct readers to focus on their personal skills, natural interests, and potential for making significant contributions rather than the uncertainties in the world surrounding them.

The first thing you must do in order to take advantage of the opportunities presented by the Knowledge Age is figure out what your unique contributions will be. You need to identify your unique combination of strengths, which Covey and Colosimo define as a combination of your natural talents, passions, and conscience.

As always, Covey is concerned with finding success through using whatever may constitute your personal set of values. For him, values, ethics, and morals are built-in motivators that can provide you and your professional activities with clear direction and purpose if harnessed effectively.

Identifying your personal strengths and unique interests enables you to write a Contribution Statement, or "a statement which sums up what you have to offer to the challenges which energize you the most" (*Bizbriefings*, Great Work, Great Career). Armed with your Contribution Statement, you're ready to take on the changing world of employment.

Before diving in and applying for jobs or sending out resumes, it's critical to first understand the new employment landscape of the Knowledge Age. Instead of simplified job descriptions and concretely defined responsibilities (these are relics of the Industrial Age), employers of the Knowledge Age want employees who can identify the company's most pressing issues and then come up with creative solutions to these issues.

By combining an understanding of your natural strengths with an understanding of what Knowledge Age employers are really looking for, you can create compelling Need-Opportunity presentations to catch the attention of a potential employer. This type of presentation outlines what a company's problems are and then describes how your unique set of training, skills, experiences, and passions will provide the best solution to those problems.

For Covey and Colosimo, these types of presentations are the Knowledge Age's iteration of cover letters, resumes, applications, and interviews. While many of these components are still part of the job-hunting process, the most powerful way to build a meaningful career for yourself — especially in uncertain economic times — is to create Need-Opportunity presentations.

The end result of approaching the job market with these ideas in mind is the ability to secure for yourself a great job: "a job where you get to use the best you have to offer — your talents, your passions, your highest ideals — to make a contribution that means something to you and to the people you love and serve" (*FranklinCovey*, Great Work, Great Career).

Throughout *Great Work, Great Career*, Covey and Colosimo consistently remind readers that the types of careers now being created in the Knowledge Age will meet both "your financial needs as well as your need to make a difference" (*FranklinCovey*, Great Work, Great Career).

Via nightthree, *Creative Commons*

Chapter-by-Chapter Summary

Great Work, Great Career

"A person with a great career makes a distinctive contribution and generates a strong feeling of loyalty and trust in others. Anyone, regardless of title or position or profession, can do these things."

- This introductory chapter provides an overall outline of the entire book, explaining its main ideas and goals. The book is broken up into two primary sections. The first section deals with defining what your unique contribution to any potential employers will be, and the second deals with what concrete actions must be made in order to see this contribution come to fruition.

- A fundamental principle of *Great Work, Great Career* is that anyone can have a great career. Building a great and meaningful career is all about leveraging your unique and personal combinations of skills, passions, and interests. And because every individual person has their own unique set of these attributes, it follows that every individual is capable of doing what it takes to create a great career.

- Similarly, regardless of where you may be at in your career—a college student unsure of what to major in, a recent graduate, or a long-time employee—the Knowledge Age presents opportunities to define and re-define yourself. Through using tools such as social networking, online researching, blogging, and even eBook publishing, anyone can become an expert and begin marketing their personal expertise to the world. In large part, this realization provides much of the excitement conveyed in Covey's and Colosimo's writing.

- Your unique contribution to the world and to any potential employers lies at the intersection of your personal talents, passion, conscience, and a compelling market need. This intersection is what will ultimately make you an irreplaceable employee, and by focusing all your interactions with potential employers on this, you make yourself an effective and attractive Knowledge Age contributor.

- At the close of this first chapter, Covey and Colosimo assert that the precise definition of a great career isn't fixed and static. Rather, it's something that's created on an individual basis. The only real requirements of a great career is that it's centered on making some meaningful contribution. Thus, Covey and Colosimo provide this loose description of a great career: *Those who create a great career for themselves are those who make the time to define their contribution and plan how they will achieve it.*

Know Your Strengths

"Most people live in a very restricted circle of their potential being. We all have reservoirs of energy and genius to draw upon of which we do not dream."

- This chapter provides the key principles to strategizing how you can become an irreplaceable employee, even when the rest of the world is experiencing widespread unemployment and frustration. One such principle is the understanding that you are a unique individual with a unique and distinctive package of strengths, experiences, talents, and ingenuity. Recognizing this becomes the bedrock for all subsequent efforts to market yourself to employers and build a great career.

- In order to identify your personal strengths—those things that will allow to present unique and compelling solutions to companies' problems—you need to take stock of your talents, your passion, and your conscience. For Covey and Colosimo these are the three components that define your personal strengths, and coming to understand them will help you better understand yourself and your potential contribution.

- The rest of this chapter is devoted to leading you through a self-inventory. To begin this introspective process, Covey and Colosimo direct you to think about your natural talents. They ask the question, *What unique knowledge, talents, or skills do you have that can help you make a contribution?*

- Next, it's time to examine your natural passions. Covey and Colosimo ask, *What job-related opportunities are you passionate about?* They point out that not all passions and marketable talents necessarily connect with one another. There may be times when a talent just doesn't really interest you, or when you may not have a great deal of talent for something that intrigues you. Despite this, there are many times when people discover their talents simply by pursuing a newly discovered passion. The key is to discover those things in life that you're both good at and passionately interested in.

- In order to think about your conscience, Covey and Colosimo pose the following question: *What is your* real *responsibility to your organization, your customers, and your co-workers?* The basic message of this section is that when you actually care about your work—when you feel a deep sense of responsibility and accountability for what you produce—then you will be a more productive, more valuable employee. This affirms that what you're doing with your time is helping you build a meaningful career.

Discover Your Cause

"Your employer or prospective employer doesn't lack problems to solve and challenges to meet. So stop thinking that opportunities are lacking—they're not."

- In the first portion of this chapter, Covey and Colosimo introduce a metaphor that is referenced throughout the rest of the book. When a massive wildfire swept through huge stretches of Yellowstone National Park in 1988, many people felt that the park had been damaged beyond repair, and all was lost. A short time later, however, it became clear that the fire actually catalyzed a new generation of trees and vegetation. Covey and Colosimo use this anecdote to point out that although there has been significant unemployment in recent years, the Knowledge Age has actually catalyzed the ability to create your own career through assessing companies' challenges and marketing your unique strengths as solutions to these challenges.

- Covey and Colosimo draw out the difference between an employee and a volunteer. They state that an employee has a job description, while a volunteer has a cause. Because job descriptions are antiquated artifacts of the Industrial Age, having a volunteer mentality—the approach that you care deeply about and are personally invested in your work—is what makes a strong employee of the Knowledge Age.

- Continuing to delineate differences between the Industrial Age and the Knowledge Age, Covey and Colosimo assert that current employers are only interested in people who offer relevant solutions to pressing problems. If a potential employee only wants a job, but can't offer a real-world solution, then that person is unlikely to be hired in the Knowledge Age.

- As the chapter continues, Covey and Colosimo pose another important question: *What is the job that needs to be done—the job only you can do?* This question is at the root of learning how to leverage your unique skills to make yourself attractive to employers. In order to answer this question, you need to conduct extensive research on the company you hope to work for. Discover as many challenges facing the company as you can. This knowledge will help you tailor your skills, training, and experience to the specific needs of the company.

This chapter concludes by explaining how to construct a Need-Opportunity presentation. This presentation combines your research and your personal strengths into a compelling statement highlighting why you should be hired. Covey and Colosimo break the Need-Opportunity presentation into three components: describe the employer's needs, describe how you've contributed to resolving similar issues in the past, and describe how you would contribute to a specific solution for your prospective employer's present needs.

The key to this approach to job-seeking and career-building is understanding that companies will never stop confronting challenges. Although the number of positions defined by a cut-and-dry job description may continue disappearing, if you know how to market yourself as a problem solver, you'll never be out of work.

Via Unhindered by Talent, *Creative Commons*

Contribute Your Best

"No matter where you are in the hierarchy of life, no matter where you are in seniority—the youngest new hire or the oldest hand at the helm—you can still make a valuable

contribution. It's a great way to work and a more fulfilling way to live."

- This chapter is all about the Contribution Statement. Covey and Colosimo define the Contribution Statement as *similar to a life mission statement, except that a Contribution Statement defines the high purpose you want to serve and what you intend to achieve in your career or in your current role.*

In many ways, the Contribution Statement is a combination of all the ideas discussed in previous chapters. Covey and Colosimo direct you to think about the attributes you most admire in influential people, consider what types of things you want to remembered for, review your strengths, review your cause, and then write it all up in a succinct Contribution Statement.

- The Contribution Statement becomes a career guide, providing direction for your professional activities. Because it's concentrated on making a meaningful contribution instead of performing a simplistic job description, the Contribution Statement becomes a critical piece in building a great, long-lasting, and rewarding career.

- After you've written your Contribution Statement, it's time to share it with others. Covey and Colosimo recommend sharing Contribution Statements with your current employers or supervisors. This will open up new channels of communication and will make clear that you're deeply and personally invested in making a meaningful contribution to the company. Similarly, if you're looking for jobs, be sure to share your Contribution Statement with potential employers to let them know that your intention is to be a real contributor and not just an employee.

- This chapter relies on the metaphor of a boat's trim tab to explain the need for every individual to make whatever contribution he or she can make. A trim tab is the small component operating between the boat and its rudder. It is what makes the rudder swing back and forth, and in turn, steer the ship as it travels through the ocean. Just as a trim tab is in itself a very small component of a much larger ship, its efforts make a dramatic difference in the overall outcome of the ship's voyage. Within a large company, it is easy to feel unimportant, but *Great Work, Great Career* asserts that when a group of Knowledge Age contributors work together, great things can happen.

- As you craft a Contribution Statement, keep in mind the difference between the job seeker mentality and the contributor mentality. As articulated by Covey and Colosimo, the difference between the two is *the difference between pushing a product and providing a welcome solution.* Employers in the Knowledge Age don't have time for unsolicited sales pitches and irrelevant resumes. But they always have time for individuals offering important solutions to current problems.

Get The Job You Want

"If you're weak in a hard moment and sleep in instead of getting up, it becomes the first of many little failures."

- In the beginning of this chapter, Covey and Colosimo remind readers that it's important to remain firmly committed to the ideas of *Great Work, Great Career* in the face of adversity. They acknowledge the fact that many companies aren't actively advertising their need for new employees. This lack of "help wanted" signs can be discouraging. To cope with this, Covey and Colosimo advise focusing attention only on what's actually within your control.

- The text outlines a difference between the Dependent Paradigm and the Independent Paradigm. Within the Dependent Paradigm, individuals see themselves as victims of uncontrollable circumstances, and they quickly lose control of their lives and their careers. On the other hand, the Independent Paradigm allows individuals to become products of their own choices. This is much more productive, as it makes it possible to take charge of the future. Subscribing to the Independent Paradigm gives you the mindset needed to create, define, and pursue a great career.

- In this chapter, Covey and Colosimo describe a system of working within your Circle of Influence—those parts of life you have complete control over such as education, effort, and personal contacts—instead of fretting over the Circle of Concern—those things you don't control like current hiring trends or economic patterns. By focusing effort on your Circle of Influence, you build up the skills and knowledge needed to become a dynamic employee in the Knowledge Age.

- As you focus on strengthening your Circle of Influence, it grows larger and more expansive. By contrast, your Circle of Concern becomes increasingly insignificant as you empower yourself to set your life's course, both personally and professionally.

- This chapter includes a passage that summarizes one of the major themes of the entire book: **No company wants to hire just for the sake of hiring, but they all want to solve problems.** This concept is what makes it possible to get hired regardless of current employment or economic trends. As long as you can market yourself as a relevant problem-solver, there will always be people and companies ready to hire you.

Build Your Own Village

"A highly synergistic team creates solutions that even the lone genius cannot foresee."

- In this chapter, Covey and Colosimo provide an updated, Knowledge Age definition of networking. In the Industrial Age past, people networked so that in times of need they would have a large list of names to use in asking for help. This type of networking isn't centered on actual relationships, only superficial introductions.

By contrast, the Knowledge Age is all about building a village of interpersonal connections and meaningful relationships. These villages are made up of professionals who share insights, information, and creative solutions together in an effort to make a real impact on the world.

- A critical component to being a part of a Knowledge Age village is contributing to the group. Covey and Colosimo suggest actively and regularly making contact with people in your networking village. Send them helpful articles or links to informative blogs. Whatever you do, be sure you communicate and share in such a way that your contacts know you're sincerely invested in the relationship.

In thinking about your networking village, it's important to note that there are two types of village members: those you serve and support, and those who serve and support you. Both types of people are critical to your success, and when you take time to really think about the roles each villager plays in your life, you'll be much more likely to contribute to finding collaborative solutions and producing collective results.

- The Internet has introduced vast new possibilities for networking, communicating, and building up your own personal village. Covey and Colosimo use this section of the chapter to discuss ways to effectively utilize social media, blogs, and eBook publishing as ways to simultaneously contribute to your valuable networking village while also establishing yourself as an expert in your particular strengths and passions. They summarize this idea by writing: *The Internet is like a great city, but you can build your own village within that city.*

- The chapter concludes with the advice to practice synergy. The authors define synergy as *1+1=3 or 100 or 1,000.* Synergy is the ultimate goal of building your own networking village. As various individuals come together, sharing ideas, brainstorms, questions, and information, the final outcome is a deep pool of knowledge and interpersonal relationships that will give each individual member of the village the tools needed to become Knowledge Age contributors.

- The concept of the Emotional Bank Account is crucial to building and maintaining a powerful networking village. As Covey and Colosimo explain it, *if I make deposits into an Emotional Bank Account with you through service, good will, small courtesies, honesty, and keeping my commitments to you, . . . your confidence in me rises, and you will come to my aid if I need you.* Of course, this Emotional Bank Account goes both ways, so that in the end, all parties involved secure strong relationships of mutual benefit.

Via johnnysam, *Creative Commons*

Frequently Asked Questions

"It's time to create your own job."

- This concluding chapter of the book provides Knowledge Age answers to some common questions surrounding the topics of job seeking and career building. Of particular importance are the sections explaining how to be effective in your use of resumes, cover letters, and job interviews.

- For Covey and Colosimo, the key to a good resume is to make it as specific as possible. Alluding to the principles discussed in the "Discover Your Cause" chapter, they highlight the need to conduct intensive research of the company you're hoping to work for. Only through this process will you be able to identify the problems for which you'll offer a solution.

After identifying the most pressing issues confronting your potential employer, tailor your resume to highlight all the ways your particular skill set, training, and experience will enable you to become a solution to the problem. In this way, resumes of the Knowledge Age are closely aligned with the concept of making a Need-Opportunity presentation; indeed, resumes may be viewed as the precursor to making such a presentation in an interview setting.

- When it comes to writing cover letters, Covey and Colosimo stress the importance of using an effective cover letter as a way of introducing yourself to a potential employer as a dynamic, creative, invaluable solution to whatever problems the company currently faces. If written correctly, the cover letter should serve as the first piece to an extended conversation that will grow to include your resume, your Need-Opportunity presentation, and finally, your actual contribution to the company as an employee.

- This final chapter provides examples of general resumes, targeted resumes, and effective cover letters. These clearly illustrate the real-world shape of the principles covered in the text.

- Covey's and Colosimo's main piece of advice for a successful job interview revolves around giving a Need-Opportunity presentation. In cases where you may not feel comfortable with this approach, they recommend the MIT Career Development Center's STAR technique (Situation, Task, Action, Result). With this technique, you relate a specific situation in which you were faced with a particular task or dilemma, you talk about what the task was, describe what actions you took, and highlight the end results of your actions. Covey and Colosimo provide a short, but illustrative example of this technique.

Closing Thoughts

"The only shortage of opportunity is in your mind. In fact, the opportunities could not be greater for those who adopt the right paradigm."

- In the book's final thoughts, Covey and Colosimo return to the metaphor of the Yellowstone National Park forest fire. They use this story to emphasize the point that in the Knowledge Age, it's up to every individual to actively and creatively build their own jobs. Through harnessing the unique talents, passions, and ideals upon which your personality is defined, and applying them to the most pressing needs of potential employers, you become a true Knowledge Age contributor. And only by contributing in real and meaningful ways will your job and your career become truly great.

- The final passage of *Great Work, Great Career* serves as a fitting conclusion, directly communicating many of the books most important concepts: *It doesn't matter if you're the CEO or the office cleaner or a police officer or a teacher or a lawyer or a waiter or a homemaker or a movie star. It doesn't matter what you do. Your career will be great if you make it great.*

Important People Referenced In Great Work, Great Career

"Don't consider yourself as a product that needs a marketing brochure. . . . Consider yourself a living, breathing, intelligent problem solver."

James Asher

A schoolteacher who invented the "Total Physical Response Method" for teaching students foreign languages. Covey and Colosimo use his story as an example of becoming a volunteer with a cause rather than merely an employee with a job description. Asher represents the authors' vision of a Knowledge Age contributor who makes real impacts simply because he chose to go above and beyond his simple job description.

Madeline Cartwright

A principal of an inner-city public school. Like James Asher, she went above and beyond her job description to develop and implement a wide array of initiatives to make her school a haven of safety and learning for her students. Her story is used in the chapter entitled, "Contribute Your Best."

Steve Chazin

A former Apple marketer who's found success as a popular blogger and eBook author. His story of success in described in "Build Your Own Village" as an example of how the Internet and other high tech devices provide increased opportunities to network, collaborate, and market expertise on a global scale. For Chazin, members of his personal village—whether potential customers, co-workers, or employers—*get a sense of who I am from the e-book and the blog in a way that a resume can't possibly deliver. There is also a sense of importance the e-book has that a resume doesn't.* Chazin's effective work online clearly illustrates the type of new opportunities becoming increasingly available in the Knowledge Age.

Julia Child

A world renowned chef and TV cooking show hostess, Julia Child discovered her talent for French cooking only after exploring her natural interest in the field. Covey and Colosimo use her story as an example of the ways that natural passions and talents can combine to create new and unforeseen opportunities for employment, income, and the chance to make an impact on the world. According to *Great Work, Great Career*, what is most important is that each individual consistently works to apply their unique sets of talents, passions, and interests to providing meaningful contributions and solutions.

Jim Collins

A well known management thinker, Collins is frequently quoted throughout *Great Work, Great Career.* Collins' work in such books as *Built to Last, How the Mighty Fall,* and *Good to Great* all focus on ways to increase personal and professional productivity. Many of the ideas and themes communicated in his books parallel Covey's own ideas and themes, making him particularly relevant to *Great Work, Great Career.* In particular, Collins provides a crucial insight when Covey and Colosimo describe the importance of allowing your conscience to play a role in defining the way you work: *One notable distinction between wrong people and right people . . . is that the former see themselves as having "jobs," while the latter see themselves as having responsibilities.*

Steve Demeter

A former ATM technician who became a millionaire after creating popular iPhone games in his free time. Demeter's story is used in the chapter entitled, "Discover Your Cause." It provides a powerful example of what can happen when people pursue their natural interests and talents, and work to discover ways to apply them to the real-world marketplace.

Ethan Nicholas

After hearing the story of Steve Demeter, Ethan Nicholas was inspired. He researched and learned how to program apps, and eventually began creating and selling his own, highly profitable line of mobile phone apps. Nicholas' story provides a compelling illustration of the importance to proactively acquire new knowledge. Covey and Colosimo write about the limitless amount of information made available by the Internet, and cites the ability to tap into this rich resource as one of the keys to becoming successful in the Knowledge Age.

Carol Eikleberry

A famous career advisor, Carol Eikleberry is quoted several times by Covey and Colosimo. One of her most well known works is *The Career Guide for Creative and Unconventional People.* In fact, Covey and Colosimo quote this book when discussing the need in the Knowledge Age for clever problem solvers: *There is no shortage of problems. Whether your problems are small or large, personal or universal, already defined or still unformulated, the creative search for solutions can be deeply engaging and even joyous.*

Charles Handy

Covey and Colosimo use the story of Charles Handy's career a few times in *Great Work, Great Career.* After years of working, Handy became disillusioned with his career. He left his job and "went portfolio," meaning he began focusing on how his unique skills and interests might allow him to become a highly sought after problem solver. After making what was initially a frightening and dramatic occupational change, Handy soon found himself making money and building a highly meaningful career for himself, using his innate skills and doing what he loved. Handy is representative of Covey's and Colosimo's vision of the Knowledge Age contributor.

William Kamkwamba

At age 15, Kamkwamba had to quit school because his family—farmers in rural Malawi— had been ravaged by drought. In response to this, he began researching and teaching himself how to build and use windmills to draw underground water to the surface and to generate electricity. His contributions revolutionized his community. In *Great Work, Great Career*, Kamkwamba's story is told in the chapter entitled, "Build Your Own Village," and it's used to point out that, *one of the greatest paradoxes of life is that the self-serving careerist never has a great career.*

Elisabeth Kübler-Ross

As a young psychiatric intern, Kübler-Ross became concerned with the way hospitals dealt with dying patients. Her subsequent work and research in this field led to the publication of *On Death and Dying.* This book became highly influential and played a central role in completely changing the way the medical world handles and thinks about death. Covey and Colosimo use her story as an example of the power to be found in focusing on the Circle of Influence instead of fretting about the Circle of Concern.

Taylor Mali

A well known spoken word poet, Mali's "What Teachers Make" is quoted in the first chapter of *Great Work, Great Career.* Covey and Colosimo use Mali's words to communicate the idea that no matter what your job, the way to build a great career is to focus on making a contribution: *A great career comes down to making a great contribution, to making a difference that matters to you and to the people you serve.*

Kathy Headlee Miner

The founder of Mothers Without Borders, Miner's story is told in the chapter entitled "Discover Your Cause." In particular, because her organization is a non-profit, Covey and Colosimo use her story to highlight the fact that *although you must make a living, your great career doesn't have to center on money*. Again, what matters most for the authors of *Great Work, Great Career* is that each individual discover ways to use his or her unique traits and personal interests to make a meaningful contribution.

Steven Spielberg

Parts of this famous movie director's life story are told in "Get The Job You Want" as an example of persevering through adversity in order to create your own job and establish yourself as an expert. As a young man, Spielberg began showing up on movie sets and volunteering to perform menial tasks. Even though nobody at the studio really wanted him around, as the years progressed, Spielberg eventually learned about the film industry. These early years of perseverance and dedication paved the way for his eventual success as a director.

Fiona Wood

As a young doctor, Wood invented "spray-on skin," a product that has grown to become a critical component of rehabilitation and healing for burn victims. Covey and Colosimo use her story early on to illustrate the power of working creatively to come up with innovative and relevant solutions to pressing dilemmas. The key aspect of Wood's story is that she refused to be limited by her job description. Instead, she became a Knowledge Age contributor by stepping outside the confines of her job, and applying her natural skills and interests toward developing a truly meaningful solution to a longstanding problem.

Key Terms & Definitions

"In all of the vast universe, there is no one else like you. You are absolutely unique. Your particular combination of strengths, experiences, talents, and ingenuity has never existed anywhere else and will never, ever be repeated. Therefore, no one else can make the unique contribution you can make."

80/20 Principle

According to *Investopedia,* this is a rule "that states that 80% of outcomes can be attributed to 20% of the causes for a given event." This rule helps "managers identify problems and determine which operating factors are most important and should receive the most attention based on an efficient use of resources" (80-20 Rule). For Covey and Colosimo, this means that you should devote most of your attention and effort at developing and utilizing those skills and interests toward which you are naturally inclined.

Abundance Paradigm

A perspective that chooses to view the world as presenting large numbers of opportunities to those willing to recognize them. According to *Great Work, Great Career*, this is the mentality of a successful Knowledge Age contributor.

Scarcity Paradigm

The opposite of the abundance paradigm, the scarcity paradigm is a pessimistic perspective that chooses to view the world as devoid of meaningful opportunities. In *Great Work, Great Career,* this perspective is associated with an outdated, Industrial Age mentality in which job descriptions are either filled or employees are fired. This paradigm lacks control and power because it views external challenges as too great to overcome. For example, an attitude of the scarcity paradigm will maintain that because so many companies are downsizing, it's impossible to get a job.

Contribution Statement

The personal statement that outlines what you will do in your current or future career to make a meaningful and significant impact on the people, lives, and activities around you.

This becomes the guide for your professional decisions and activities. In order to write an effective Contribution Statement, you must consider what your natural strengths are and how these will allow you to become a critical piece to your current or prospective employer.

Cover Letter

For Covey and Colosimo, the cover letter is your chance to start a conversation with your potential employer. It should demonstrate that you've done your research, that you're familiar with the challenges faced by your potential employer, and that you've already formulated a solution. A cover letter should make a potential employer want to continue the conversation by reading your resume or inviting you in for an interview.

Emotional Bank Account

Life Training – Online defines this as "one of the most powerful ideas ever created for the development of interpersonal relationships" in which you build up a strong "account" of positive feelings, trust, and support by engaging in sincere acts of service and communication (The Emotional Bank Account). The concept of the Emotional Bank Account helps place the focus of networking on building up genuine relationships rather than amassing a long list of unfamiliar names.

Industrial Age

For Covey and Colosimo, the Industrial Age is the most recent paradigm of economic production, and is characterized by the use of human beings as tools or small parts of a larger production machine. This is an outdated mode of production, and will not lead to great careers in today's world. Under this paradigm, employees were fully defined and restricted by overly simplistic job descriptions.

Knowledge Age

This is the current mode of economic production, and it relies heavily on the increased communication and technology of the Internet and other technological advancements. Under this paradigm, human beings are viewed as unique contributors to an ever-changing world of problems, questions, and dilemmas. In order to keep up with the shift from the Industrial to the Knowledge Age, individuals must learn to market themselves as problem solvers and big time contributors.

Need-Opportunity Presentation

The way in which you communicate to a potential employer the contribution you will make to his or her company. The key is to point out a problem the company is struggling with, then use the presentation to "illustrate the impact of the need and the opportunity you represent" to overcome the problem (*FranklinCovey Solutions,* Need-Opportunity Presentation Planner).

Generic Resume

A generic resume "acts as a foundation on which to build job specific"—or targeted —"resumes" (*Job Search Skills,* Generic Resume). Covey and Colosimo recommend using a generic resume to help identify the best information and personal data to use when crafting a targeted resume, and later on, a Need-Opportunity presentation.

Targeted Resume

According to *About,* a targeted resume "is customized so that it specifically highlights the experience you have that is relevant to the job you are applying for" (Targeted Resume). For Covey and Colosimo, an effective targeted resume serves as the precursor to the Need-Opportunity presentation.

From X To Y By When

This phrase is used to describe the need to quantify, as much as possible, the various components of the contribution you plan on making at a particular company or for a specific potential employer. In the equation, X refers to the current situation of the company or employer, and Y represents where the company or employer will be when their current problem is solved. This is where the effective and savvy Knowledge Age contributor comes into play. By describing to a potential employer what her current predicament, "X," is, and how your actions, "Y," will help her company succeed, you capture her attention. The final component is to provide an estimate, "By When," regarding the time frame in which your actions will solve your employer's challenge. If you can give each of these variables concrete and measurable figures, you stand a great chance of delivering a powerful Need-Opportunity presentation.

Job Interviews

As discussed by Covey and Colosimo, the traditional idea of a job interview is in flux, along with the rest of the job-seeking, career-building process. While job interviews still occur regularly, the authors of *Great Work, Great Career* recommend using the interview as a chance to make your Need-Opportunity presentation. If this doesn't work for some reason, you should use the STAR technique: tell your potential employer about a difficult situation you had to confront, what your specific task was in solving the problem, what actions and decisions you made, and what the results of them were. The key lesson regarding interviews is to understand that *interviewers no longer ask if you have the skills they want—they now ask you to tell them about specific instances when you used your skills.*

Job Seeker Paradigm

This concept is the approach taken by employees and workers of the Industrial Age when trying to get hired. In it, workers view themselves as products to be marketed and sold through generic resumes that function as advertisements. Covey and Colosimo view this paradigm as ineffective because it essentially places potential employees in the position of asking employers, *Because I need a job, will you please hire me?* Instead of proactively creating jobs and solving problems, the job seeker paradigm forces individuals to rely on strictly defined skill sets and extremely limited job descriptions, both of which have become outdated in the Knowledge Age.

Contributor Paradigm

This is the predominant attitude of the Knowledge Age contributor. Individuals who function within this perspective understand that companies today are seeking out people who can help them solve problems and who can adjust to the ever-changing demands of a global marketplace. The contributor paradigm embraces a proactive stance in which employees view themselves as dynamic solutions rather than prepackaged products. Instead of presenting potential employers with bland resumes, a contributor paradigm employee makes Need-Opportunity presentations and demonstrates to employers just how valuable his unique combination of skills, talents, and interests are.

Knowledge Worker

According to the traditional definition of this term, a knowledge worker is "engaged primarily in acquisition, analysis, and manipulation of information as opposed to in production of goods or services" (*Business Dictionary*, Knowledge Worker). In the work of Covey and Colosimo, this term is expanded to include any employee who seeks to make meaningful contributions by creatively working to identify and address the challenges, problems, and questions raised by a complex and global economy. This type of individual is typically contrasted against the Industrial Age worker of the past, who's entire career was defined by the strict limitations of a very specific job description.

Solution Conversation

Instead of sitting down for a job interview, Covey and Colosimo suggest turning your interview with a potential employer into a solution conversation—the discussion in which you will make your Need-Opportunity presentation. Before having a solution conversation, it's critical to do whatever research is necessary to familiarize yourself with the problems faced by that employer. This will then allow to use your experience, training, skills, and passions to market yourself as an individual capable of solving your potential employer's challenges. In short, *describe the need they have and how you can help them meet it.*

Win-Win Performance Agreement

As defined in *Great Work, Great Career* a win-win performance agreement is a description of *what would be a win for the organization and a win for you personally.* These types of conversations are especially effective when you find yourself trying to maintain a job while also struggling with feelings of career stagnancy. In order to rise out of the occupational doldrums and begin making truly meaningful contributions, Covey and Colosimo suggest coming up with some unique solutions you can offer your employer, and then sharing these ideas in a win-win performance agreement.

Interesting Related Facts

"You don't need to have the most thrilling, high-profile job in order to make a great contribution and to love your work."

- Stephen R. Covey is a member of The Church of Jesus Christ of Latter-Day Saints (*Freebase*, Stephen Covey).

- Jennifer Colosimo's blog persona is "Executive Mama."

- The idea that recent years represent part of the Knowledge Age is not unique to Covey and Colosimo. Social theorists and academicians have been using this term, along with the associated "knowledge worker," for years.

- Jennifer Colosimo is a National Delegate for Girl Scouts of the USA.

- Covey has received four honorary doctorates for his work in business, leadership, and time management training (*White Dove Books*, Biography of Stephen R Covey).

- *Great Work, Great Career* mistakenly refers to spoken word poet Taylor Mali as a woman in the book's opening chapter.

- Stephen R. Covey's oldest son, Stephen M.R. Covey has made a name for himself as an influential business mind with the publication of his book, *The Speed of Trust.*

- Stephen R. Covey is a recipient of the Thomas More College Medallion for continuing service to humanity (*White Dove Books*, Biography of Stephen R Covey).

- As a follow-up to *Great Work, Great Career*, Covey and Colosimo teamed up to release *Career Advantage: Real-World Applications From Great Work, Great Career.*

- According to *White Dove Books*, Covey's book, *First Things First,* is "the best-selling time management book ever" (Biography of Stephen R Covey).

Sources Cited

"Pay the price to know your facts cold. If you take such an approach with decision makers, you will get their attention and blow them away with the depth of your preparation and discipline."

- *White Dove Books*, Biography of Stephen R Covey

- *Premiere Speakers Bureau*, Jennifer Colosimo Bio

- *Business Book Summaries*, Great Work, Great Career

- *Bizbriefings*, Great Work, Great Career

- *FranklinCovey*, Great Work, Great Career

- *Investopedia*, 80-20 Rule

- *Life Training – Online*, The Emotional Bank Account

- *FranklinCovey Solutions*, Need-Opportunity Presentation Planner

- *About*, Targeted Resume

- *Job Search Skills*, Generic Resume

- *Freebase*, Stephen Covey

- *Business Dictionary*, Knowledge Worker

- *Jennifer Colosimo*, About Jennifer

Additional Reading

"Finding the job you want is 90 percent research!"

- *FranklinCovey Consultant Blogs*, Book Review: Great Work, Great Career by Covey and Colosimo

- *Stephen R. Covey*, Blog

- Career Advantage: Real-World Applications From Great Work, Great Career

- *The New York Times*, Top Author Shifts E-Book Rights to Amazon.com

- *Jennifer Colosimo*, Blog

Table of Contents

I. Quicklet on Stephen Covey's The Leader in Me: How Schools and Parents Around the World are Inspiring Greatness, One Child at a Time

Quicklet on Stephen Covey's The Leader in Me: How Schools and Parents Around the World are Inspiring Greatness, One Child at a Time

About the Book

"I like the idea of putting quotations up and I also liked the idea in the book of hallways labeled with a street sign of one of the 7 Habits...We need to build a culture of not just talking the talk but of actually walking the walk." The Leader in Me – Chapter Responses

Published in 2008, Stephen Covey's *The Leader in Me* revolutionizes public education and brings many people to the table who see potential, and invest in youth. *The Leader in Me* surpasses established schoolroom formulas and empowers students, teachers, parents, administrators and business people lead the preparation of this generation to "thrive in the 21st century." According to Covey, the book was born out of need to make his 7 Habits of Highly Effective People applicable to students in primary grades. The book, or rather the *7 Habits* system, is rapidly growing in popularity in schools around the world. Covey wonderfully captures the system's successes and challenges in *The Leader in Me*.

About the Author

"As the father of nine and grandfather of fifty, he received the 2003 Fatherhood Award from the National Fatherhood Initiative (NFI), which he says is the most meaningful award he has ever received." Champions Club Community

Covey's honor from NFI, coupled with a life long passion for teaching leaders and for enabling communities to develop one person at a time, is the bedrock of his philosophy. Writers at Success Magazine credit Covey with having an "all star" resume and describe him as an "effective leader and one of the most sought after voices in business, education and government."

Covey received an MBA from Harvard, a doctorate from Brigham Young University and was inducted into the Sales and Marketing Executives Hall of Fame (SMEI) in 2000. Among other achievements, he also received the McFeeley Award from the International Management Council for significant contributions to management and education in 1991.

Covey's parents "*constantly confirmed his worth and potential even as a young child*," and have affected his success and leadership a great deal. The writers at Success Magazine also report that Covey was the oldest child (a natural leadership position) and was mentored by his grandfather, an entrepreneur and leader in the Mormon church. That early life exposure to business and to doing business with principles shaped Covey.

Covey is attentive and focuses on people who believe that existing situations can be changed. Covey is a change agent who loves being in the company of other change agents. The evidence of this characteristic is best expressed in a later Covey work called The 8th Habit.

Overall Summary

"Indeed, it is my sincerest hope that this book will somehow spread its figurative wings and soar with a reach that will truly make a difference in the lives of young people the world over—now and for generations to come."

After a very impressive seminar on the *7 Habits of Highly Effective People*, a fiesty elementary school principal named Muriel Summers approached Stephen Covey and asked him if 7 Habits could be taught to kindergarteners. Covey told Ms. Summers to call him if she ever decided to try to teach *7 Habits* to kindergarteners . Since Summers needed a miracle to turn her school around she gathered up a school team and developed strategies for getting 7 Habits into the hearts and minds of her pupils. *The Leader in Me* is robust with the details of Summer's journey to becoming the number one magnet school in America.

In his Huffington Post blog, Covey summarizes the strategy that worked at Summers A.B. Combs Elementary.

"The principles of effectiveness are creatively woven by teachers into every subject — reading, math, history, science, social studies, art, etc. From the moment they walk into the school each day until the final bell rings, the children soak in their adult leaders' belief that they are leaders of their own lives, have unique talents, and can make a difference. Each child, including those with special needs, is given a leadership role in the school: leader of greeting, leader of public speaking, leader of the school's daily news program and so forth. They love it and they thrive."

"Thrive" is an understatement considering Summers' reports of dramatic increases in test scores, enrollment, student self-confidence, teacher and parent satisfaction, as well as business and corporate support. Discipline problems have significantly decreased.

In *The Leader in Me* Covey breaks down the process of implementing *7 Habits* at Combs into small steps. Then Covey gives us glimpses of some of the strategies that worked in schools in other states as well as in Canada, Guatemala, and Japan. In his 2010 Huffington Post blog, Covey reports that over 200 schools have participated in the *Leader in*

Me process.

Since integrity is one of the principles Covey emphasizes throughout the book, it is certainly no surprise that he admits to being challenged by cynics and naysayers along the way. The cynics, he reports, have a problem with his theory that all children can be leaders. Covey has a ready answer for that group.

"We don't define leadership as becoming the CEO or the few percent who will end up in big leadership positions. We are talking about leading your own life, being a leader among your friends, being a leader in your own family. Leadership, as one school put it, is doing the right thing even when no one is looking."

Watchman Fellowship at Apologetics Index.com has some significant concerns with Covey's program. In an article entitled "*The Shifting Paradigms of Stephen Covey*", the writer Bob Waldrep contends that the *7 Habits* may not be suitable for Christian homes and churches because of "*problematic conflict with biblical doctrine*." Waldrep presents a strong case, but more importantly leaves Christian readers and parents in general with some sound advice concerning wholesale acceptance of a program that seeks to instill values in our children: be very careful and exercise discernment.

"Like others, Christians seek that which will help them overcome problem areas. As we seek such or help others in their quest, we must be very careful, exercising discernment

*as to whom and what we endorse; remembering not all that offers a solution to life problems is of God. (*1 Thessalonians 5:21 ↗2 Corinthians 11:13-14 ↗; Matthew 7:15 ↗ ; Proverbs 14:12 ↗*). If it does not pass the test of Scripture it is of no profit and should be avoided."*

Covey customizes his program to meet the specific needs of the target group. He would likely take Waldrep's contention in stride without a great deal of debate. In fact, Covey devotes the book's final chapter to thoroughly discussing the role of the family in educational reform.

The bottom line for Covey, in his work, and especially in *The Leader in Me* is that children be properly equipped to meet the demands of a 21st century society, both in terms of character and competence. Fortunately for us, he doesn't mind moving on every possible front to disciple others to do that equipping. Several of his children are already on board and he challenges us to get with the program.

Chapter by Chapter Commentary and Summary

Chapter One: Too Good to be True?

If we are putting all of our efforts on the almighty test score alone, I am quite afraid that we are going to create a generation of children who know how to do nothing but take a test well. **—Muriel Summers, Principal, A.B. Combs Elementary**

In this chapter Covey sets the tone for and gives us a sneak preview of the case he will make in favor of leadership-centered rather than fact-centered education for all children. From his perspective, we have to look at the present offerings in schools today and see if those schools are adequately preparing young people to thrive in a 21st century marketplace. For Covey that preparation is a partnership principally between schools and parents who can join forces and send the same message to young people. Covey presents his pilot leadership training program through the eyes of a parent searching for a good neighborhood school.

The pilot for Covey's '*Leader in Me*' program is A.B. Combs Elementary in Raleigh, North Carolina. The statistics, the reputation, and the word of mouth about Combs Elementary is so extraordinarily positive that the parents have to visit to see for themselves. Their visit to Combs is eye opening and answers the question in this chapter's title, "Too good to be true?"

From the moment they step on campus, these parents get an opportunity to experience Covey's '*Leader in Me*' program at work. The parents witness four keys that distinguish Combs from other schools.

1. The school is clean and the writings on the walls (graffitti) are uplifting and motivating

2. Students are genuinely confident and respectful in their dealings with peers as well as adults on campus

3. Teachers are energized and able to engage their pupils in a variety of challenging

learning activities

4. Students are involved in problem solving and critical decision making on every level at the school.

Of course, the visiting parents were so impressed with both what they had seen and heard that they immediately enrolled their children in Combs.

Covey is quick to let us know that his "*Leader in Me*" program is a viable and sustainable program that is being customized and practiced in schools internationally. Customization is an important feature of the program because Covey wants schools to adapt the timeless universal leadership principles in '*Leader in Me*' but to also to bring the special flavor of each community into the process.

Covey also wants readers to view the success stories of the model programs he will share in depth in later chapters through the lens of each program's ability to

- honor the universal leadership principles
- bring out the best in each individual child
- promote parent teacher partnership in transferring values

The great bonus for '*Leader in Me*' is that businesses are seeing the value of the program and are providing independent funding to assist schools in impacting the workplace of tomorrow.

Chapter Two: 'What Parents, Business Leaders, and Teachers Want from a School

"They wanted children to grow up to be responsible, caring, compassionate human beings who respected diversity and who knew how to do the right thing when faced with difficult decisions."

It really does take a village to raise a child capable of thriving in the 21st century workplace. What has to happen is that the village must point a collective finger to the village and hold the entire village responsible for its young people.

In this chapter Covey delivers a moving testimony through the pen of A. B. Combs, school turnaround specialist and current principal, Muriel Summers. Covey inserts an occasional comment, but for the most part it is all Summers and that's all good.

Summers recounts a powerful story of surveying the village stakeholders and putting in place a new school mission. That mission was a new beginning for the school and the sure pathway to the school's becoming one of the most imitable schools in the world. The mission was simple: develop leaders one child at a time.

The year was 1998 and Summers' boss gave her one week to turn around the fledgling magnet school which had little or no drawing power. Summers first gathered the stakeholders at the fulcrum of the situation: the parents. She quickly discovered that parents were not at all concerned about academics. Instead, they were more concerned about their kids walking away with the soft skills necessary to get along with their peers and to make something of themselves.

After consulting with the parents, Summers turned to her own staff to see what teachers wanted for the school. Teachers were clear. They wanted to impact their students in much the same way that special teachers in their lives impacted them.

Next, Summers and the Combs staff rounded up business leaders to hear their advice on the workforce of tomorrow. She discovered,"Most business leaders know all too well that deficiencies in both character and basic life skills in their employees are costing their companies dearly every day and they are desperately hoping that schools can help out in both regards."

Summers then considered the results of checking in with students, and weighed her question from the Covey seminar on the *7 Habits of Highly Effective People*: Can these 7 Habits be taught to young children?

With the schools future on the line and the needs of the village gathered, Summers answered the question. She proposed a new school theme, a new mission that embraced T*he 7 Habits*.

A.B. Combs Elementary School has never been the same. In fact, the rebuilt magnet school has nearly tripled its student body and draws an abundance of top-notch applicants for open teaching positions. Combs also draws visitors from all over the world who desire to see leadership training at its finest.

Chapter three: 'Crafting a Blueprint for Leadership'

"Our school's vision is To Live, to Love, to Learn, to Leave a Legacy."

With a vision and theme in tow, the Combs team needed a specific strategy to deliver the leadership principles to students, staff and parents. They had to come up with a way to teach and simultaneously integrate the core principles of *7 Habits* into everyday activities at Combs. Here's what they did step by step:

- 'Begin with the end in mind' and establish 21st century skills as their schools' measurable outcome.

- Build on solid ground infused with

  1. genuine caring, loving and respect

  2. wanting the best for students

  3. strong committment to discover and unleash the gifts in each child

- Build a twofold foundation based on Covey's habits and Baldridge's tools

  1. Teachers learn, teach and give students opportunities to practice Covey's *7*

     Habits of Effective People–"Be proactive, begin with the end in mind, put first

     things first, think win-win, seek first to understand then be understood, synergize

     and sharpen the saw."

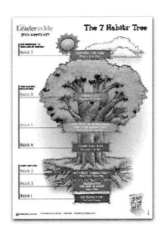

  2. Incorporate Baldridge tools as the other strategic part of the school's

     foundation.

     Baldridge enabled the team to focus on measurable outcomes, tap into best

     practices in education, chart progress and engage students in doing the same.

Baldridge was the U.S. Secretary of Commerce in 1981 and was responsible

for exposing educators to tools traditionally used to make organizations
more
effective.

"These principles were shared openly, and were intended to help leaders

improve their decision-making, problem-solving,efficiency, and innovation
skills.

Some of the tools had been around leadership circles for years, such as

force-field analysis, Venn diagrams, bar charts, and fishbone diagrams.
Others

were less familiar, such as lotus diagrams, spider matrices, and bubble
maps."

- Adapt current best practices and update regularly.

Writing the vision on the walls of the school as well as in the hearts of the entire Combs
community became a win-win for all.

Chapter Four 'Aligning for Success'

My immediate thought after reading chapter three was that A.B. Combs could not have
possibly been an overnight success. Systemic change is a term I hear a lot in nonprofit
community development circles and the resounding cry is always that this kind of change
takes time. That was the case for Combs and Covey illuminates the challenges of bringing
forth systemic change at Combs in this chapter.

There were four areas the Combs team needed to focus on.

"1) Bringing people "on board" with the new theme

2) Aligning the school's structure to match the strategy

3) Training the staff in the 7 Habits and quality principles

4) Aligning the reward systems so that the right outcomes would be reinforced and sustained."

Bringing adult stakeholders on board was the greatest challenge. Rather than force the new system on teachers, as an example, Summers launched a pilot program and when other teachers saw the results in test scores and student behavior they bought in. Similarly, when parents with kids in the pilot program witnessed results they told other parents and so on and so on. Community and business leaders, as well as school district personnel couldn't help

but hear the buzz and they too came on board. Business leaders went a step further and showed their support by investing dollars in the program.

Because this reform needed to be woven into the very fabric of the school, roles had to change. In effect, everyone on campus had to take on a leadership role and be held accountable for their specific area of responsibility. Teachers and students alike were engaged wholesale in "unleashing the potential in each child." Students got the experience of applying and interviewing for school wide positions and many were even included in interviewing new staff.

Modeling was the great outcome of the staff training. Combs staff learned to practice what they preached and became living, breathing ambassadors for both *7 Habits* and the Baldrige principles. "*As a staff, they became committed to utilizing the tools in running the school and each classroom, and in holding themselves accountable."*

The final challenge was aligning reward systems with the new way of life at Combs. Staff decided that creativity and hard work should be emphasized and that exceeding expectations in these categories should get the high marks. Over time the Combs staff was united in insuring that students knew that people at Combs were rooting for their success and were available to help.

Covey did not fail to include a note about the other side of rewards and indicated that consequences for bad behavior also was also included in Combs' recipe for success.

Even the naysayers and skeptics could not deny the empirical and anecdotal evidence resulting from reforms at Combs. Clearly its mission to draw out the best in all who are involved qualifies it to be rightly called a magnet school.

Chapter Five: Unleashing a Culture of Leadership

A school's "culture" results from the combined behaviors of the people involved in that particular school. It is sometimes referred to as "the way we do things around here."

Just as in the previous chapter, Covey reminds us that the success of Combs happened over a sustained period of at least a decade. It was a process, to say the least, and when the time came to launch, everyone was on the edge of their seats. Covey refers to that special piece of Combs history as a major "leap of faith" mainly because Combs was the pilot program.

Covey gives us an insider's tour of the working of the plan through the lens of a lay anthropologist. His tour begins with the first day of school and he shows us the reformed *"behaviors, language, artifacts, traditions (rituals), and folklore"* that an anthropologist would study.

- First, Covey shows us an academic free first week of school. Instead of academics, teachers engage students in connecting with the 7 Habits and with each other. *"They talk about accountability.They have students create, apply for, and interview for class and school leadership roles. They set personal and class goals and assemble their data notebooks. They have students help write classroom codes of cooperation—what behaviors "are" and "are not" acceptable.They create artwork to go on bulletin boards..."*
- Next, Covey shows us Comb-ese, the campus language. *"We dwell in possibilities here." "We tell them we love them every day." "We focus on what they can do, not what they can't do." "We focus on the positive." "Every child is important."*

    Words like these along with the *7 Habits* are written on the wall, spoken over the

    school's intercom, sung, acted out, taught and incorporated into every aspect of

    Combs life.

- As for artifacts, classrooms and hallways are laden *"with creative ideas and displays, but the key is that they all reinforce the leadership theme and class goals."*
- Traditions are established that, of course, reflect and reinforce the vision, mission and philosophy of the school. These include special events in individual classrooms as well as for the entire school, including a Leadership Day, an Inaugural Ball and

    an International Festival.

- In the way of folklore, Covey recounts the numerous stories, mostly success stories that demonstrate the impact of the *Leader in Me* program on the Raleigh, North Carolina community.

Chapter Six: Rippling Across the Globe

"Today's business world is very competitive, and most businesses operate on a global basis. To be competitive you have to have a strong foundation of people skills. If we can have the habits developed at this early age, these children will truly be the leaders and the good employees of the future. So it is truly an investment in the future." – Rick Redmond, Vice President, Criterion Catalysts and Technologies, Canada"

In this chapter Covey turns our attention to the broader picture and allows us to see the *Leader in Me* program in diverse places. Covey's goal is to show the "unique twist" each of these schools have put on the program and to further prove that his template for building tomorrow's workforce works.

First, Covey takes us to schools in the continental United States and he shows us the impact on behavior and morale.

"One of the keys to the success of the leadership theme is that teachers love teaching the material to students. It is visible in the teachers' eyes, and they are very creative in how they go about it. In a day where we hear so much about bullying going on in schools, what a great process and moment this is to see kids respecting each other. —Dede Schaffner, Seminole County School Board

"Most notably, discipline referrals dropped from 225 the previous year to 74 the year following. And, according to the annual climate survey, parents' approval of the school rose to 98 percent."

Next, Covey takes us to Canada and shows us the possibilities of school corporate partnering.

"When a local business learned that Crestwood was teaching the 7 Habits, its employees approached the school with "How can we help?"

"Today's business world is very competitive, and most businesses operate on a global basis. To be competitive you have to have a strong foundation of people skills. If we can have the habits developed at this early age, these children will truly be the leaders and the good employees of the future. So it is truly an investment in the future." – Rick Redmond, Vice President, Criterion Catalysts and Technologies, Canada

Covey's final thought is summed up in what he terms a school's signature, a quality that he says must be present for *Leader in Me to work.*

"This is not an off-the-shelf program that teachers stand up and regurgitate verbatim. First they must live and love the 7 Habits and other leadership concepts. Otherwise students will feel the duplicity. But more than anything, they must attach their own personality—their own voice—to what they are teaching. They must make it their own. When they do, it shows up in their eyes, in their language, and in the way they handle discipline matters. At that point, the students begin feeling it and believing it."

The question is how much rippling can public education stand? The answer is found on the blog at leaderinme.org and at seancovey.com. New results come in regularly and effective February 2012, the *Leader in Me* program is being implemented in 500 schools worldwide.

Chapter Seven: Moving Upward and Beyond

"The foundation of every state is the education of its youth." – Diogenes Laertius, quotation on ceiling of Joliet Township High School Central auditorium

Covey opens chapter seven with words that capture the importance of a village truly embracing its youth. As the title indicates, the move was first upward from elementary schools to junior and senior high schools and then beyond to international sites.

While Covey focuses on the *Leader in Me's* impact on elementary school students in previous chapters, he takes us to some junior and senior high school campuses "to provide a glimpse of what is happening at those levels—and there are some great things happening. There are also some interesting things happening at district and government levels that I will briefly introduce at the end of the chapter."

A tiny spark of The *Leader in Me* was ignited in Joliet, Illinois at a moment where a high school counselor named Tony Contos was fed up with the educational system. Contos wanted desperately to make a difference on campus but his efforts were repeatedly thwarted by school bureaucracy and red tape. A colleague insisted that he read the *7 Habits* book. Contos not only got excited, but he was able to see connections between the *7 Habits* and the problems his counselees were experiencing. He took a leap of faith and reached out to Covey to see if there were lessons and exercises suitable for high school students. There were no programs for teens at the time, but Contos began to experiment with students and staff and got wonderful results.

Once again, parents saw their children begin to change and wanted to know who or what was responsible. Parents discovered that the culprit was a set of principles contained in a book called *7 Habits* and they began to get excited. As the good news about 7 Habits began to circulate in the community a unique funding opportunity became available. A representative from the District Attorney's office offered to give the school a portion of the proceeds from confiscated goods found at drug raids.

Shortly after Contos' pioneering efforts to deliver the principles to teens in Illinois, Covey's son Sean wrote and published *7 Habits of Highly Effective Teens.*

"Since its release,The 7 Habits of Highly Effective Teens has sold over three million copies and traveled to schools all over the world, including a classroom in Korea where students are learning a 7 Habits song with actions."

According to Covey, getting junior and senior high schools to implement the *7 Habits* program was a tremendous challenge mainly because of curriculum requirements.

Still, the concept of empowering teens, especially low income teens was very attractive. A cluster of schools in Chicago offered the program in a mandatory class for incoming freshmen. Additionally, each freshman is assigned an advisor for the entire four years. The advisors are trained in the *7 Habits* and are able to integrate the program into their advisory sessions. Even without a full immersion in *7 Habits* the schools report increased test scores, decreased disciplinary issues and a greater propensity to attend college. A pilot program in California has also experienced a similar impact.

Covey's most exemplary high school program is at Roosevelt Junior High in Oklahoma City. Marilyn Vrooman, the incoming principal, describes Roosevelt as a school where the "halls were filled with young students whose academic lives were drowning in social issues they were not equipped to handle."

Vrooman attacked the problem on two fronts: the facility first and then the faculty.

She discovered some special interests the students had and designed student hangouts around those interests. Her intent was to to give them opportunities to experience interpersonal communications in customized settings.

She also took the advice of a book entitled *If You Don't Feed the Teachers They Eat the Students!* and built a faculty exercise room. She empowered the teachers with the *7 Habits* training and allowed them to incorporate the training into as many student lessons as they saw fit.

One especially significant campus innovation involved a group of young men.

"She received a $10,000 donation to fund the building of a ropes course for teaching leadership skills and hired a contractor to work with fifteen at-risk boys to design, build, and install eight low-level rope elements. The experience allowed the young men to gain a confidence in themselves that they were then able to transfer to their coursework."

Covey admits that Roosevelt is "not paradise" but it certainly is on the upswing.

The *Leader in Me* program's impact is certainly not restricted to the United States. Covey reports amazing results from Singapore, Guatemalan and Japanese schools. In Singapore, for years the trainings were exclusively held for teachers and there was no systematic attempt to bring the program to the students. At the insistence of parents, in 2000 Covey and educators combined forces and developed a Highly Effective Youth (HEY) program that has positively transformed the school culture for adults and youth.

Covey is particularly proud of his accomplishments in Guatemala. In 2005, the minister of education responded to what seemed like an epidemic of national hopelessness by implementing a program called Path of Dreams.

"The more she and her team synergized, the more María came to believe that the habits would empower both teachers and students to "relearn how to dream" and provide them with the tools to make their dreams become a reality."

Path of Dreams is working and the take away for youth and adults is a burning desire to improve themselves and the country at large.

Covey's *7 Habits* program has literally swept Japan and although it was initially a 'hard sell in a tough school system' the results are really extraordinary.

 "Today more than ten thousand students a year receive the 7 Habits via cram schools, while another three thousand receive training in the habits from private schools. Since parents must pay for cram schools and private schools out of their own pockets, I believe this says something about what parents in Japan want from a school."

Covey ends the chapter by emphasizing the growing list of corporations, community groups and school districts contributing to a 7 Habits culture.

"I share the Louisville and Dow Agro Sciences stories—and single out their activities—to emphasize how interested community and business groups are in the well-being of today's young people and how important they find these basic life skills and principles to be."

The uncanny thing about this transformation is the culture shock students experience when they graduate or go into a 7 *Habits*-free environment. For Covey that culture shock may be just the driving force necessary to take his program to yet another level.

Chapter Eight: 'Making it Happen, One Step at a Time'

"But if change is difficult for a solitary individual, how challenging must it be for an entire school?"

In this chapter Covey gives readers a blueprint for implementing a leadership theme. He calls the process "The Four Imperatives of Leadership" and reminds us that success depends on customizing the process to meet the needs of the school.

- **Inspire Trust**

- **Clarify Purpose**

- **Align Systems**

- **Unleash Talent**

For Covey, inspiring trust and building quality relationships are hallmarks of successful leadership programs. Additionally, many people are afraid of or reluctant to change because unchartered territory is frightening. Covey suggests that the only way to inspire trust is to prove trustworthiness and to develop trusting relationships with those we serve. "People will not care how much you know until they know how much you care."

That is certainly sound thinking, and it explains why leaders like Martin Luther King led from the trenches. People saw King making sacrifices and practicing what he preached.

People will trust a leader when they believe they are heard and cared for. They also have to know that a leader is true to his or her word.

"That trust has to be present for desirable change to happen in a school."

The second imperative Covey insists on is clarifying purpose. His definitions for terms we hear everyday are worthy of noting here.

- mission: the purpose
- vision: the destination
- strategy: the path
- job expectation: the specific roles each individual will play

The third imperative is aligning sytems. A great example is the human body with every system working cooperatively toward one end. What a design! Then too, when one body part gets weak other parts rush to the scene to take up the slack. Metaphorically speaking, when a person goes blind. Ears always rise to the occasion.

Covey breaks down the aligning into four areas–*attracting, positioning, rewarding and developing people.* Here's what it looks like from a human resources point of view.

- attracting: recruitment (internal)

- positioning: placement (right adults and youth in the right jobs at the right time)

- rewarding: Incentives & accountability– *"How will progress and successes be rewarded? How will people be held accountable for inappropriate actions?"*

- developing: training. "It is in the actual "process" of teaching, creating lesson plans, designing displays, and leading school events that teachers, students, and parents best learn the leadership principles**."**

The fourth imperative is unleashing talent. There is no room for insecurity here because this is the principal's or the director's opportunity to strategically delegate. Covey reminds us that leadership is an enabling art and that great leaders know how to stir up the gifts and bring out the best in every member of the team. He writes, "this applies to more than teachers. It applies to unleashing the talents of parents and community volunteers, but particularly to unleashing the talents of students."

Covey's final thought here has to do with sustaining the change. He strongly recommends reevaluating, and refreshing and most importantly keeping the main thing the main thing.

Chapter Nine: Ending with the Beginning in Mind

"Any person who unlocks the unseen potential of others and inspires them toward noble causes is a modern-day miracle worker."

Covey unleashes his best argument yet for getting the reader to buy into the *Leader in Me* program. What Covey is hoping for is for us to realize the tremendous difference that can be made when we treat each child like a diamond in the rough waiting to be mined. Who would dare argue with that noble intent?

For Covey, raising up leaders is not only a worthy investment, but should be the primary focus of our educational system. What's more, he would have us to believe, effective leadership training must come packing the following elements:

- a mission to equip students to thrive in the 21st century
- a will to make caring a school tradition
- a sharp knife to cut out the non-essentials and to make room for incorporating the mission in the core of every school activity
- a village-centric attitude that will insure that educational reform fits the specific needs of the village

"Today's young people may not be ready to run multinational corporations upon graduation, but they should at least be able to effectively make basic life decisions, to feel a sense of worth, to walk with confidence, and to dream. What greater thing can we do than to meet them at their crossroads and do our part in enabling them to lead their lives?"

That's the challenge for we who occupy the village. Whether we rise to that challenge is up to us.

Chapter Ten: Bringing it Home

"But, nowadays, so long as a home is within reach of a wireless signal, every cubic inch of that home's airspace is infiltrated with potentially destructive messages and images that can steal away the identities—particularly the moral identities—of young people."

Bringing it home is a suitable theme for this final chapter and an opportunity for Covey to reflect on the role of the most sought after stakeholders in the village–the parents.

Parent buy in to any youth program is a challenge that has to be tackled. Covey does not give the reader any magic formulas for engaging parents, but he does suggest that parents will definitely pay attention when their children bring home new and improved behaviors. Covey has a wealth of evidence to prove that leadership development via the *7 Habits* does indeed bring about a behavior change. So, school leadership teams should definitely be prepared to train parents as a part of their strategy.

The training for parents, as for other stakeholders, should be rooted in a belief that–*"if you treat all students as if they are gifted, and you always look at them through the lens of being gifted in at least some aspect, they will rise to that level of expectation."*

Covey offers several questions that should be raised at parent trainings, as well as five watchwords that will align the parents with other stakeholders.

Questions to Consider

- *"What gifts does this child possess naturally?*

- *What talents or character traits does this child possess that if nurtured a little more could turn into gifts?*

- *What gifts, if any, did this child possess at an early age that have since been muted by his or her cultural DNA?*

- *What have I said to this child within the past three days that has communicated my recognition of his or her gifts?*

- *What will I say to her or him within the next twenty-four hours that will communicate my recognition of and admiration for those gifts?"*

Terms

- Affirm: teach correct principles-Model what you want your children to catch
- Inspire trust: clarify purpose–align ousehold systems–unleash talents
- Write a family mission statement: stay on course–go at the right pace–keep it simple
- Teamwork: Build independence and interdependence
- Teach and reward character and contribution

List of Important People

Covey refers to all of the movers and shakers who are bringing this viable program to their various communities as modern-day miracle workers. The list is too long to include here and in each community it is the whole team effort that makes *The Leader in Me* process work.

Key Terms and Definitions

- Primary greatness vs secondary greatness.

Covey defines primary greatness as character and contribution

Secondary greatness is wealth, awards, positions or fame

"Financial success—prestige, wealth, recognition, accomplishment—will always be secondary in greatness," Covey says. "Primary greatness is about character and contribution. Primary greatness asks, What are you doing to make a difference in the world? Do you live truly by your values? Do you have total integrity in all of your relationships? And when correct principles are not followed or ignored, the result can be catastrophic as we have witnessed the past year in the financial markets."

- Leadership: "Leadership is communicating people's worth and potential so clearly that they are inspired to see it in themselves."

- Ubiquitous: Woven into or permeating the very fiber of person, place or thing. A good example is a toddler with a melted chocolate on his or her hands. We can be assured that that chocolate will get on every thing or every person the toddler touches.

Interesting Related Facts

- Stephen Covey conducts seminars for the American Management Association (www.amanet.org)

- Stephen Covey's son, Sean has also written books- including The 7 Habits of Highly Effective Teens and The 7 Habits of Happy Kids

- Stephen Covey is the cofounder and vice chairman of Franklin Covey Company, a consulting firm with the slogan–We enable greatness in people and organizations everywhere.

- Covey's book, The 7 Habits of Highly Effective People was published in 1987 and has been on the New York Times Bestsellers list.

Sources and Additional Reading

- Simonandschuster.com, Stephen Covey:Biography

- Coveylink.com, The Leader in Me

- Sources of Insight, Lessons Learned from Stephen Covey,

- Stephencovey.com, Press Release

- Mormonwiki.com, Steven R. Covey

- woopidoo.com, Quotes by Stephen Covey

- Success.com, Coveted Wisdom

- Academy of Achievement, Stephen Covee, Honoree,

- stephencovey.com, Stephen R. Covey Blog

- Apologeticsindex.org,The Shifting Paradigms of Stephen Covey,

- Leader in Me at DE Smith & WA Porter, Blogspot

- Combses.wcpss.net,The Leadership Model

- Seancovey.com, Educators

- The LeaderinMe.org, Articles and Case Studies

About the Publisher

Hyperink is the easiest way for anyone to publish a beautiful, high-quality book.

We work closely with subject matter experts to create each book. We cover topics ranging from higher education to job recruiting, from Android apps marketing to barefoot running.

If you have interesting knowledge that people are willing to pay for, especially if you've already produced content on the topic, please reach out to us! There's no writing required and it's a unique opportunity to build your own brand and earn royalties.

Hyperink is based in SF and actively hiring people who want to shape publishing's future. Email us if you'd like to meet our team!

Note: If you're reading this book in print or on a device that's not web-enabled, **please email** books@hyperinkpress.com with the title of this book in the subject line. We'll send you a PDF copy, so you can access all of the great content we've included as clickable links.

Get in touch:

Made in the USA
San Bernardino, CA
02 July 2013